MASTER YOUR LIFE

MASTER YOUR LIFE

TO THE 10TH DEGREE

Bendecido Books Inc.
A DIVISION OF WE COMMUNICATIONS WEST INC.

Master Your Life to The 10th Degree

Copyright © By Glen Daman

Published by Bendecido Books Inc.
A division of We Communications West Inc.

For more information address:

Bendecido Books Inc.
A division of We Communications West Inc.

7 – 1080 Waverley Street
Winnipeg, Manitoba, Canada R3T 5S4

www.bendecidobooks.ca
www.wecommunications.ca

Library and Archives Canada Cataloguing in Publication

Daman, Glen

Master Your Life to The 10th Degree – 1st ed.

ISBN 978-0-9812045-2-9

Mixed Sources
Cert no. SW-COC-001271
© 1996 FSC

Printed and bound in Canada

To Donna Justin and Brandon, you are the reason for everything in my world. When I open my eyes each morning you are the ones I think of first. When I close them at night, you are the last thought of the day. Thank you, all of you, for your patience and advice. Thank you all for sitting in the front seats of my bus. Simply put I couldn't live the 10th Degree without you in my life. I love you all very much.

"Play your music loud, Dance like no one is watching and dream large! Live days with vibrancy, surround yourself with people that have passion and have conversations that call out your best inner self. Elevate your world everyday! Have a 10th Degree day."

- Glen Daman

TABLE OF CONTENTS

CONGRATULATIONS, YOU PURCHASED THIS BOOK. YOU'RE ON YOUR WAY TO THE 10TH DEGREE.

Congratulations! Welcome to the 10th Degree and the best decision you ever made in your life! The first step to reaching the 10th Degree is simply your decision to pick up this book. Naturally, you're standing there and asking yourself, "Why should I read this?"

Well, I won't waste your time: Let me ask you a few questions:

- Do you find it hard to get up each morning because you have no motivation for the day?
- Do you have a hard time sleeping at night because you are worried or anxious?
- Do you struggle with relationships?
- Do you struggle setting goals for yourself and then find it difficult to focus on those goals.
- Do you always look at the negative in life as opposed to the positive?
- Do you struggle with your emotions?
- Are you cranky all the time? Do you struggle with your attitude?
- Do you want to find a way to enjoy life?

If you answered "Yes," to at least three of these questions, you're probably desperate to read this book. If you answered "Yes," to just one of them, I'm convinced I can fix your problem.

The 10th Degree is a Five Step Program designed to give all of us our best life. I can't make you rich, that's up to you, but I can provide you with a plan to make your career a success. I can't guarantee that you will marry the girl or boy of your dreams, but I can give you the tools to have successful relationships.

It was the brilliant American businessman, investor and Midwestern prophet (or would that be profit?), Warren Buffet, who said: "there will never be a better you than you," and I certainly agree with Mr. Buffet.

However, while it's easy to say "Be the best you can be," somebody has to show you how. In this book, I'll show you how.

It's not easy, but then again, it's isn't terribly difficult either. As I will explain pretty consistently on the pages of this book, if it wasn't easy, I wouldn't do it. The key is to get started.

To help you remain on top of the steps and to remember everything you believe is important to you, I've added a number of note pages at the back of the book. Don't be afraid to use them.

I guarantee that if you follow my five easy steps toward the mastery of life's five most important elements, you will reach the 10th Degree and you will have the tools required to live the life of your dreams.

No one is going to give you a great life. Only you can do that. However, if you live a 10th Degree life, all of your dreams will be within reach.

WHO IS GLEN DAMAN AND WHAT IS A 10TH DEGREE LIFE?

Glen Daman grew up in a trailer, the son of a single mom trying to make ends meet, in rural Manitoba. It wasn't your silver-spoon start to any journey, but Daman was a guy who wasn't going to finish last in life's race.

In fact, the youngster who grew up with virtually nothing, went on to become president of a large Canadian automotive group and is, today, managing partner of Winnipeg Hyundai. You'll learn a lot more about Glen later in the book, but suffice it to say, his entire life has been the answer to his favourite question: "Why wouldn't you?"

Glen approaches everything in life with a great attitude, absolute honesty and with a sense that "Yes is the answer, now what was the question?"

A business executive, salesman, trainer, father, husband and friend, he's also a sought after speaker and life coach.

However, on the way to becoming a great salesman and successful executive, Daman also developed an approach to life that makes every day a great day – whether life wants you to have a great day or not.

Called the 10th Degree Life and based upon the teachings of the word's greatest salesmen and finest martial arts masters, Daman will take you through the disciplines of Physical Mastery, Mental Mastery, Emotional Mastery, Professional Mastery and Relationship Mastery, and show you how to make the absolute best of whatever hand you've been dealt in your life.

If you've seen him live you know that there are very few speakers in the world more dynamic – and entertaining and fun – than Glen

Daman. He'll get you "All Geeked Up" and ready to make the best of each and every day, just by following his easy five step program to what he calls, "The 10th Degree Life."

You too can live a 10th Degree Life and make every day a 10th Degree day. In this, Glen's latest book, *The 10th Degree Life*, he'll take you with him on the most wonderful ride you can imagine and help you live life to its fullest.

But there is one catch: You must give him 60 minutes a day. It will make you better, make your business better and make your relationships better. In the end, it will make your life better.

- Scott Taylor

ALL I'M ASKING FOR IS 60 MINUTES A DAY

After years of development, after speaking to countless numbers of people in many seminars, my 10th Degree program has morphed into an extremely simple process. And make no mistake, it is a process.

Based on my life experience and some of the principles of martial arts, I have combined this knowledge with the countless numbers of books I've read (by authors such as Robin Sharma and Og Mandino) and seminars I've attended (presented by the likes Paul Cummings and Joe Verdi), to come up with a program that is absolutely guaranteed to make you a better person and give you a better life. If you simply attain the first degree, your life will improve noticeably. Get to the 10th Degree and your life will improve significantly.

In this book, we will discuss attitude, set you on your way toward getting "all geeked up" (we'll explain more about that later) and actually explain how your life is just one big bus.

But first, let's talk about the principles.

The 10th Degree is a combination of five distinct steps which have been divided into The Five Books of The 10th Degree: Book 1, Physical Mastery; Book 2, Mental Mastery; Book 3, Emotional Mastery; Book 4, Professional Mastery; and Book 5, Relationship Mastery.

In order to reach the 10th Degree, I'm going to ask you for 60 minutes a day. It's not for me. Not by a long shot. It's for you.

You give me 60 minutes of your day – almost all of it before your regular day starts – and I will guarantee you a life of happiness and success. No, I can't make you wealthy beyond your wildest dreams, but this book will make you rich – rich in you relationships, rich in your approach to every day living and very, very rich in your attitude toward the people around you.

This book will give you knowledge and wisdom. And if you follow it, you will feel so good about yourself that you will be amazed how that feeling influences everything around you. In fact, you'll ask yourself "Why didn't I do this years ago?"

But remember, no shortcuts. You must follow the outline. Book 1 relates to Book 2 to Book 3 and so on through Relationship Mastery. If you keep to the program, it's foolproof. The 10th Degree won't happen overnight, but it will happen.

Here's what I need you to do. I want you to take just 60 minutes every day. And remember, this is all for you:

Book 1: Physical Mastery
- Walk/dance/do pushups
- Get the blood flowing and creating energy
- Create your own energized environment

Book 2: Mental Mastery
- Read something positive, not negative
- Remember: as we think, we are
- Positive in. Positive out
While we read, remember to eat a well balanced diet

Book 3: Emotional Mastery
- Focus on all the positive in your life.
- Remember to "Count to 10"
- Hold the line

Book 4: Professional Mastery

• Focus on your goals, daily

• Tie your goals to your dreams.

• Remember, your day is made up of activities not tasks.

Book 5: Relationship Mastery

• Who do we want on our bus? When we make the decision are we nurturing those relationships?

• Wealth should be measured by our friendships.

• Count your blessings every day. Focus on the people who love and care about you.

There you have it. If you go through these exercises, exercises that we will explain in great detail in the coming pages, you will immediately improve your life.

Now, remember if you add time to each section there is absolutely no penalty. These are minimums. Frankly, we recommend that you live the 10th Degree for every waking hour. Concentrate on the mastery that gets you to the 10th Degree and not only make yourself great, but the people around you as well.

However, if you leave a step, at any time, it will penalize you. No, you aren't going to lose yardage, or go to the penalty box, but because every step relates to the next step, leaving, say, physical or mental mastery out of your daily routine will not go unnoticed by you.

The 10th Degree is your life. It's not mine or his or theirs. If you follow the steps, each and every day, you will feel the rewards. No, they won't necessarily come to you in the guise of fast cars and wheelbarrows full of money, but the rewards will be yours to enjoy. You will feel better about yourself, better about the people around you and you will develop the most loving, caring relationships that you have ever known.

The 10th Degree is about personal responsibility and personal success. And if you live it, you will have a rich, positive life. But it will not only make you better, it will also make your friends, loved ones, schoolmates, fellow employees and the institutions and companies you work all that much better just for having you around.

OK, now is the time. It's on to the 10th Degree.

THOUGHTS ON MASTERY

"A black belt isn't just something you put around your waist. It's how you live your life."

- Master Malcolm Edwards

The dictionary definition of the word "mastery" reads as follows:

"The acquisition or the process of acquiring proficiency in an aspect of spiritual practice. Command: great skillfulness and knowledge of some subject or activity. Domination: power to dominate or defeat. The act of mastering or subordinating someone of something. The position or authority of a master: dominion, command, supremacy, superiority. Full command of some subject or study."

For many people, the term "mastery" is something that is directly related to the martial arts and I would agree that's very true. And yes, I have been interested in martial arts mastery for much of my life.

However, to be "a master" does not necessarily mean you have to master the kicks, punches or weapons of the many martial arts disciplines. While martial arts is an interest of mine, this not a martial arts book and while the teaching of the martial arts prepares you to master its skills, so too do many other professions.

Think about it. What is the most prestigious of all golf tournaments? The Masters. What do you have when you finish your first post-graduate degree? A Masters degree. If you complete a course at one of the world's finest culinary schools and you have the experience, you're a Master Chef.

This book is about mastering every aspect of your life. In fact, I guarantee that if you follow the steps as outlined in this book, you will become a master of your body and mind.

But remember, when you finish this book, you may have reached the 10th Degree, but your work doesn't stop there. As Master Edwards of Bae's Martial Arts once told me, "When you reach your black belt, most people think you've finished your training, but that's not true. It's only just beginning."

I'll give you the tools. I will provide you with the means to master your life. But when you have all those tools in your tool box, you must put them to work every day. That's how you become a Master. That's how you live a 10th Degree Life.

FOREWORD

By Bob Sadler, BEd; BA (Hons); MEd

I don't need help. None of us do. At least that's what we try to tell ourselves. If this was the actual case, why then do so many of us reach out to alternate ways of achieving our life goals? Why do we pick up motivational books like this one and incorporate the ideas into our supposedly great life style?

The answer is we do it because we aren't confident, successful or able to handle our life stressors in the way we feel society, our families, and friends and ourselves feel we should. If I am wrong, I apologize. Why then did you pick this book off the shelf, open it, and continue to read this far. You may be a friend and merely want to patronize the author, but I think you have other reasons. I think there is more.

You probably need to be motivated to work through the challenges of life's complexities, as well as satisfy your psychological and emotional needs through self-actualization, or the fifth level on Maslow's Hierarchy. This is the level that deep down inside we all hope to achieve in life. It is the level, however, that few manage to attain. Many do not get past the basic needs in life, never mind achieve self-esteem and beyond. Basically, everyone wants to be as successful as they possibly can be, but few know how to get there on their own. We all want to be rich: Physically, emotionally, mentally and professionally. If we didn't, we wouldn't have heroes, buy lottery tickets, read self help books and we wouldn't keep living through dreams of Utopia. This is what makes us human. We all want the best for ourselves and our families just like all animals in the species.

For you who have opened this book and read this far you will find it is another motivational "Self Help" discourse. However, this book is like no other. It is not written by a man who spent years at university or someone who is a noted therapist. It is written by a

19

self-made man who is like a son to me. He is also a very dear friend who I have seen take people from the depths of despair and turn them into very successful citizens in our community.

He has also risen out of his own rock bottom and gone on to achieve greatness in life. Glen Daman is an individual who learned to be successful on his own, by reading, learning from the best and taking what he internalized and turning those ideas into successful strategies. Glen could have gone to levels of higher education but he chose a unique path of his own. Instead he followed his family's tradition and went into the car industry. Glen wasn't born rich, not materialistically, but he was born rich in ideas and energy.

All his life, he wanted to be successful and thus he became one of the few that make it to a level that many dream of, but only a few attain. The best part is that he did all of this before he was 40-years-of-age.

Driven by his passion to succeed, Glen went from car sales to management quickly. Within a short period of time his skills were so honed that he became the president of a conglomerate of car dealerships, but this was still not enough to satisfy his quest for success. He then left that position to pursue ownership in his own dealership, finally taking his skills on the road to become a top motivational speaker and sales trainer. This, ladies and gentleman, is a self-made man who knows what he is talking about when he eloquently discusses his life secrets.

This book takes a look at what made Glen successful both professionally and personally. Some of these ideas you may have heard about before, but Glen's thoughts on attaining the upper echelons of success are straight forward concepts that I have seen used with many an individual. For more than thirty years I have professionally assisted people who have succumbed to levels of despair. Dutifully, I have followed many of the great theorists, but I have never seen success like I have when I utilize Glen's rhetoric on life. This is a man who has used what he preaches, not only to assist others, but to help them reach a high level of self-satisfaction, which in turn helps them overcome adversity and life challenges.

Not only has he done this in terms of his own career goals, he has done this as a successful family man who is a devoted father and husband. Glen, along with his wonderful wife Donna, raised two successful sons; one who is a top athlete and scholar the other who is ASD or autistic. Both have reached levels that most parents wish their own children could achieve. This is something that takes courage and commitment to one's own beliefs and convictions.

But, understand, the concepts divulged in this book are not something that Glen Daman has used all his life. They are strategies that have been developed, revamped and fine-tuned over years. Glen quickly learned in life that wealth can only come when one opens their eyes to a diversity of ideas and incorporates them into their own tool box of successful strategies. This knowledge he has imparted to all who will listen. And those who do, have been amply rewarded.

When you get to know Glen through this book, you will realize that he has become a life long friend of those he touches. All my life I have never seen him shun an individual or give up on them because of their inability to make successful life decisions. He doesn't look at life as one big baseball game in which the premise "three strikes and you are out," can be taken literally. In fact, many that have worked with him over the years have been on a roller coaster of successes and failures. If they didn't they wouldn't be human. The secret is how you handle the speed bumps of life. Some give up, of course, but successful individuals do not. They look around and say, "What is next?" They want to know what they learned from what just happened, and what can I do different the next time.

If you want to reach your own level five on Maslow's Hierarchy or the tenth on Glen's you need to set goals and rigorously commit yourself to following the ideas. If you do, I can guarantee success and so will Glen. This book thus becomes one man's journey and his rise to the top.

You have three choices: (1) You can wallow in self-pity, hoping life will eventually deal you a miracle. (2) You can be satisfied with mediocre or (3) like Glen, you can be the best you possibly can be, rising to a level never before experienced. The choice is yours and only yours. All of us are dealt different cards in life, but it is up to each individual to incorporate their own idealisms and strategies into the life long climb to unique and self fulfilling prophecy for which we all want to be remembered.

INTRODUCTION

By Troy Westwood, 17-year member of the Winnipeg
Blue Bombers of the Canadian Football League

Most of us know someone who, when they walk into a room, reminds us that they indeed have a piece of the sun somehow in their soul. These are people who emanate a kind of positive energy that everyone can feel.

This is Glen Daman.

When Glen walks into a room you can sense there is something special about him. When you hear Glen Daman speak, whether it is to hundreds during a motivational speech, or if he is talking one on one with you about his family, there is an undeniable, tangible passion in every single word the man speaks.

Glen Daman has a gift. He calls his gift the 10th Degree. The 10th Degree is all about living and understanding life to its fullest. Of course, Glen does this in all facets of his own life.

I have known Glen for 15 years. I have watched him live his life as a husband, a father, a businessman, and as a friend. Glen's approach to life is contagious. I have been very lucky over the years to know that when I needed to speak to someone to ask for advice, or to gain a different perspective, I could call Glen and listen to his interpretations on a wide range of life's experiences. There wasn't a single time in all of the times I approached him that I didn't come away with a deeper understanding of the situation at hand. There wasn't a single time that I didn't come away inspired.

Live life to the fullest. We have all heard the phrase. We have all tried to apply it to our own lives. Many of us can live life to the fullest for short spurts, before we slip back into something else. Something that is short of our potential, something that is not living our lives to the fullest.

Imagine what we could accomplish if in all facets of our lives if we could maintain the pace of living life to the fullest, the pace of the 10th Degree?

This is the essence of the 10th Degree. The 10th Degree isn't a "sometimes thing." Once you come to a deep understanding of the teachings, the 10th Degree becomes a part of every breath you take, a part of every action you make. The possibilities of what you could achieve, if at every moment of every day you were living the 10th Degree, would be endless.

Here is the secret. You hold the key to the 10th Degree. Read this book. Devour this book. Commit yourself to the message in this book and the payoff will be far-reaching and life-altering.

We all have the power within us to make ourselves better through the decisions and choices we make. Allow yourself greatness. Take yourself to the 10th Degree.

THOUGHTS ON MY FRIEND, GLEN DAMAN
By Lee Goren, SC Bern (Switzerland) Hockey Club

In November 2005, I was living in Vancouver, British Columbia, when I received a random telephone call. At the time I was in the fifth year of my professional hockey career, playing with the Vancouver Canucks of the National Hockey League. This random call came from a gentleman would end up becoming one of my closest and dearest friends.

Glen Daman's eldest son, Justin, had just made Canada's national Karate team. As a reward Glen had decided to take Justin to a Vancouver Canucks hockey game. Part of the reward, as it turned out, was having dinner with fellow Winnipegger Lee Goren (As the Lee Goren in our story, I'm not sure if that was part of the reward or not).

Glen and Justin chose to attend a game in January. Unfortunately for all of us, I was sent to the minors on New Year's Eve. However, on the upside, I was sent to the Canucks American Hockey League affiliate, the Manitoba Moose.

When Glen and Justin returned to Winnipeg we talked about the possibility of getting together for dinner and even spending a little more time together. Glen and his family, his wife Donna and sons Justin and Brandon invited me over for dinner and drinks. They have not been able to get rid of me since.

In the four short years that we have been friends I have seen a lot of qualities that Glen possesses that are truly admirable. His people skills are one of his greatest assets. He is so welcoming and easy to get along with, very giving and caring. He has a wonderful family that he cherishes and adores and it's a warmth that I have witnessed time and time again. He is not only enthusiastic but sincerely excited about every aspect of his life, and that enthusiasm carries over into the lives of his friends and family. There is not a day that goes by that Glen Daman is not giving 100 per cent of himself in every phase of his life.

Glen was blessed with a son, Brandon, who has Autism. Brandon is 16 and is in high school and the way Glen interacts with that boy is nothing less than remarkable. Brandon is the apple of his eye. Glen is the president of the Autism Foundation of Manitoba and helps the organization raise money for programs designed to help children with Autism.

During the summer of 2009, I was given the opportunity to witness Glen's abilities first hand. He and I – OK, mostly him – organized a charitable golf tournament to raise funds for Autism Manitoba. It was our "first annual" and together – OK, once again, it was mostly Glen – we raised more than $40,000 for Autism Manitoba. It was truly remarkable just watching Glen put his many talents into action and I marveled at the skills he can use in all aspects of his life.

Glen is a motivational speaker and life coach. He is not only one of my best friends, but he is the person I turn to with most of my questions and concerns about life. But I'm lucky. I get plenty of face time with Glen and I always look forward to those times. Whether it is putting together a golf tournament or just having dinner, I know that I am in for a good time with a great friend. And I just might learn something, too.

In the four years that I have had the privilege of getting to know Glen I have seen him run a multimillion dollar business, without losing sight of the importance of spending time with family and friends. I can tell you this from the bottom of my heart: The 10th Degree is for real!! Glen does more than just talk about living; he is an example of how we should all live our lives. Every day. Striving with a smile and a helping hand to be the best we can possibly be.

GLEN DAMAN: A LIFE

"Glen Daman? He's always up, always friendly, always ready to encourage, not to tear down. He has integrity. He is trustworthy. He's demanding, but never petty. To know him well is to know a real friend, a friend with a golden heart and a friend who has a clear, committed approach to living the 10th Degree life. And to think, he grew up in a trailer on the edge of a farm with an often-absent dad. He's a remarkable human being."

- Scott Taylor

WHO IS GLEN DAMAN?

Glen Daman started with nothing and became a success.

It's a story we've heard many, many times before, but this one rings with so much heart and love, that it's what bad movie scripts are made of.

Glen, the third child of Koert and Anita Daman, had nothing but love. It's a story that's far too melodramatic for modern cinema. It is, in many ways, saccharin sweet.

The Glen Daman we know today is outgoing, powerful, insightful and, if you've heard him, you know he's a brilliant speaker. He's also a successful businessman, a tremendous husband and father and a man who gives his time for those who don't have the same benefits, both physically as well as mentally, that most of us do.

He is an ideal citizen and a man who will, inside the pages of this book, change your life for the better – if, in fact, you want your life to change.

But we'll get to all that soon enough. Right now, let's meet the man who lives a 10th Degree Life every single day. Let's find out where he came from and how he got to where he can now stand before you and tell you the secrets of productivity, love and happiness that have made him successful, not only in his professional and family life, but also in his relationships with those around him.

This is Glen Daman. This is the first step on the road to the 10th Degree.

- **Scott Taylor**

BEFORE I GOT ALL GEEKED UP!

"It's not where we come from, it's where we are going."

- Glen Daman

I grew up in an incredible household, surrounded by love.

When I tell you my story, it might not sound like that, at least not on the surface, but it was true. My mother did everything she possibly could for my brother, my sister and I. We didn't have much growing up, but we had love.

I grew up in a trailer on 5 acres in rural Manitoba, a parcel of land owned by my grandparents, on a portion given to my mom and dad.

There were three of us kids: my brother Gordon was born in 1968, my sister Karen was born in 1970, and I was born in 1972. My parents were having terrible marital problems in our younger years. My dad is an alcoholic, reformed today, but an alcoholic, nonetheless. My dad was never really with us, he left for good when I was about 10, so we never really had any money, and my mom raised the three of us pretty much by herself.

She worked as a bank teller – and bank tellers don't get paid all that much. She had three kids and a mortgage, in a trailer. And that mortgage, by the way, was paid sporadically. My mom constantly fought the wolves at our door and there were times when I would open our fridge and not seeing anything inside.

I remember my mom being so upset that she couldn't give us more, but what she gave us was actually everything, because we really survived on love alone. She was my mom and my dad and my best friend all rolled into one. She tightened my skates, she washed my clothes and she cooked my meals. She did everything.

One of my favorite memories of having fun with my mom and my siblings was actually a pretty simple thing. Every Friday night we would sit around the television and watch Dallas. Mom would make popcorn and we would have family time with the Ewings!

We very seldom had soft drinks or potato chips in the house, so popcorn was a favorite, inexpensive treat. On special occasions, or when mom had a few extra dollars, a large bottle of Coca-Cola would wind up in our refrigerator and that was a very big deal.

Family time was extremely important in our house. After all, we could not afford big outings so time at home was huge part of our social lives. We had fun playing a variety of card games and board games were a constant, Monopoly was the favorite. As we got older, all of our friends would join in. I have great memories of a time back when I was 16, finishing my shift at a local gas bar at 11 pm on a Friday or Saturday night and mom would have the game board set up and friends would be over when I got home. We would play until 2 or 3 am.

Back then, I was a decent hockey player and mom figured out a way, every year, to have me play hockey. And whether you live in Canada or the United States, you know how expensive that is. Granted it was 1982 and hockey sticks were $20 not $200 because they were made of wood and when you're breaking one or two a game, well, my mom had to "find a way".

There were always people around who would give me rides to the rink and make sure I got to practices and games. On those mornings when games or practices were really early, I would stay at other players' houses for the night.

One thing, in that community we always had friends and that's something I will never forget.

Now, remember, we're living on a farm, but we're not farming. It's my grandfather's land and he's retired and can't work it anymore so he's renting it out. That means my mom didn't make any money off the farm.

However, what my mom did receive from the farm was support. She had her in-laws, my grandparents, right next door and to their undying credit, my grandparents treated my mom like their own daughter, even after she separated from my dad. My grandparents were truly amazing people and, quite often, were more like real parents to us than just grandparents.

They lived in the main house on the farm which was located only about football field's length away from our trailer. I was in their house every day of my childhood. My grandfather died in 1995 and it still is the saddest day of my life. I miss him dearly. Not surprisingly, he motivated me to write about death many years after his passing: "When you experience the pain of loss, whether it's a family member, friend or significant other, find comfort in knowing that the connecting thread in all of them is love. The love that is stored in your heart. Even though they have left our ground, they will rest forever in our hearts, never to leave again."

Although my family didn't work the farm, I did chores for my grandfather and my brother did have some chickens, so we always had a few eggs. However, other than eggs in our fridge, there were times that there was little else. I can remember my mom waiting for payday to "restock" the pantry so three bowls of cereal or soup in a day comprised our breakfast, lunch and dinner.

I understand there were, and still are kids, who have it worse. The 10th Degree Life that I try to live today forces me to remind everyone of this. When I think of this, it makes my mom's trailer seem like a palace. Even though living in that trailer was often stressful and draining on my mom, I wouldn't change a thing about those days. They are a very big part of who I am today.

We went to school in a small town outside Winnipeg, and despite all my hardships at home, I was a pretty popular kid at school. That's because I had two things going for me: I was a decent athlete and I was the class clown.

We all have ways of dealing with adversity. My way of dealing with absolutely everything – not just adversity but everything -- was humor. So I joked about anything and everything and if I could make people laugh, I was happy. Gordon dealt with it through religion. He found a number of Christian youth groups and became part of that scene, which is awesome as far as I'm concerned. That was his escape.

Karen and I were close growing up so we hung around with a lot of the same friends and she had her group of friends and combined with my group of friends, we both got a lot of support. Our friends were everything then and are everything today.

As we got older, things started to get a little easier. Mom got promoted at the bank, Gordon went out and got his own job and started to help out and then Karen and I got a job and suddenly everyone was doing better.

I know where I came from. I came from a trailer on the edge of my grandfather's farmland in rural Manitoba. I started with nothing, but the love of my family and a belief that I was smart enough and good enough and maybe just funny enough to make something out of my life.

And the best part was knowing it was all going to get better because I was going to have the right approach to life, the right attitude every day, to make it better.

I didn't know it then, but because of everything that happened to me in that trailer, I was going to discover the 10th Degree.

MOMMY'S BOY, DAD'S MAN

I have no trouble admitting that I was always a mommy's boy. I loved my mom for every little thing she did for us and we were close, very close.

I did, however, look up to and love my dad. I was ashamed as a child in school not having a mom and dad together. I wanted so badly to have my dad at home like the other boys in my class. I wanted to have my dad take me to hockey games, both my games and the games played by my beloved Winnipeg Jets of the NHL.

But dad was always gone and I felt as though he didn't want to be with me. My dad and I had a very tumultuous relationship and as I entered my early, and grew into my late teens, I directed a lot of negative energy toward him.

Then things started to turn around for us and it got significantly better after I was married. I had obviously matured a great deal and I realized I shouldn't be blaming my dad for everything that had happened in the past. My understanding of alcoholism and relationships grew the longer I was married.

When our first son Justin was born, my dad told me he was going to quit drinking. I'd heard it before and I had my doubts, but told him I would support him and this time it was different. He kept his promise.

Today I seek my dad's advice on almost everything. He uses his life experiences, not only to help me but many other people. My dad is a terrific grandfather - to all his grandchildren - and today, he is one of the best dads I could have ever hoped for. I say this with all sincerity, he is one of my best friends. I speak to my dad daily and could not imagine my life today without him.

When I was 15, I got a job pumping gas at a popular local outlet and with all the kids now working (and finally paying for some of our own things); my family was acquiring a little more money. Still, I had to get a ride to work every day in Winnipeg, where the gas station was located about 20 minutes away. But by now, Karen and Gordon had their own cars, so there was always a ride available when I had to go to work.

Meanwhile, back at the trailer, our place was becoming Grand Central Station. Everyone loved my mom and we all had plenty of friends and our little trailer became a centre of activity. As we grew into our teens, our friends would stay all the time. To this day, half of my friends don't call my mom, "Mrs. Daman," or even "Anita," they call her, "mom" which is a fitting tribute to her.

I look back on it and while I know we were poor, my upbringing was awesome. Considering that until I became old enough to work, I had virtually nothing and I think that's what made it great. As I reflect on my own life and success as a grown up looking at my own kids, and my children have all these things and all these opportunities in life, I wish they could spend a couple weeks living the way I did as a kid. We always say we want to appreciate what we have, and I firmly believe it becomes more difficult to truly appreciate how great your life is.

There was a party for my mom when she retired from the Royal Bank and my brother Gordon told one of the most moving stories about her. When he was 15 or 16, he earned a spot in the Manitoba Youth Parliament. Well, he did such a great job that he was asked to go to Ottawa to take part in Canada's National Youth Parliament. The problem was that it was going to cost $300, money that that my mom did not have and she was too proud to ask anyone in the family for help. My mom was always careful not to involve the extended family with her hardships. She was so independent. She had nowhere to turn, everything was already taxed to the max - credit cards, loans, everything was completely tapped out. But her boss at the bank loaned her the $300 dollars with an overdraft on her chequing account. She paid it back and through it all, proved to me how great it is to have friends, to never burn bridges and always do well by people, because eventually they will do well by you. I didn't know it then but she was the first person to show me the importance of Relationship Mastery.

At my mom's retirement, my brother wrote her a cheque for the $300 and said, "Mom, thanks for always doing anything and everything for us." There wasn't a dry eye in the house and to this day she still hasn't cashed it!

One of my mom's favorite performers is the country legend George Strait. Not long after she retired, I made arrangements to secure a private box suite at the MTS Center in Winnipeg for the concert. Everything was catered, my mom was treated like a Queen and all I did was stand behind them with my wife, and I started to cry. I looked at my wife and I said, "Honey, now I know I've arrived at where I want to be." To be able to do this for my mom was a dream come true. She deserved it - and so much more - for all she did for me and Gordon and Karen.

ON THE WAY TO GETTING ALL GEEKED UP

At 16, I bought a K-car. My dad worked at a local used car dealership and sold me the car and co-signed my first car loan.

I made the payments, bought the gas, kept it tuned up and

running all by myself. All on the money I was making at the gas bar and chicken catching in a nearby town.

In rural Manitoba, we have these large barns, many with 10,000 or more chickens. Every so often, the farmers would have to empty the barns as the chickens reach their maturity for egg laying. As teenagers, we would be hired by the farmer to reach in the cages pull the chickens out put them in crates to be shipped out for soup and other uses. It was great money but really hard work.

So here I was, chicken catching and pumping gas, and then I started delivering pizza at Dominos. I had it made. I was going to school, living with my family in our trailer and working multiple jobs. Life was just great.

But I wanted something more. I wanted the coolest job in the world. I wanted to be in sales. I wanted to wear that striped referee's jersey and be involved in sports. I wanted to work at Footlocker.

I got dressed up and went to the Footlocker at a large mall and walked inside and said, "Hi, I'm looking for a job and I've got a resume."

He said, "I'm sorry, but I'm not the guy who does the hiring, Ray does. But he's busy right now."

"That's okay, I'll wait," I said.

I waited around for quite sometime and finally, out comes Ray and he says, "Sorry son, we're not hiring."

"Well, that's too bad for you."

And he laughs and says, "Why would you say that."

"Because I'd be the best 16-year-old salesman, not only in this city, but in this province and in this country," I said.

And he laughed again and said "You're really sure of yourself."

"Yep, and there's only one way you can find out how good I am. You have to hire me to find out."

At that point, he's getting a little perturbed and he said "I'll tell you what I'll do. I like you. Let's go sit out and sit on that bench in the mall." He said, "Tell me a little bit about yourself," so I said I'd work harder than anyone you'd ever met, you wouldn't be sorry you hired me and you'd be so happy, you would tell everyone that you hired Glen Daman.

He looked at me and said, "Alright, you start next week, but you're working in the stock room." So I stocked shoes for a few months before he gave me the chance to sell and he finally let me on the floor and I never went back to the stock room. It was unbelievable. I was a salesman at 16 years old. And to this day my friend, Ray, will tell you that I kept my promise, just like I told him I would.

I had no idea what a The 10th Degree Life was back then, but I knew I was on to something and I knew it all started with me, it started with my attitude and how I approached every single day of my life.

DONNA

It was the first day of grade 11 and Donna Duckett's life would change forever. I didn't say for the better but definitely forever.

Growing up, David Stott and Brett Hachkowski were my best friends and we all went to high school together. The other friend, more of an adopted brother really, was Mark Pelletier. Even though we all grew up together, he went off to a private school in Winnipeg that my son Justin now attends. So he was not involved in the "school life."

David and I were typical Grade 11 hockey jocks and we're both class clowns. Mr. McMillian was our homeroom teacher.

So we walk into class and, we're late of course, because we were always late, and I look at David and I say "Whoa! First day! Grade 11 and look at that, there's a new girl in the class."

I walk straight over to her and I said "Hi, I'm Glen and you're in my chair." And I sat right on her lap.

Right away Mr. McMillian says "Daman! Please give her a break! She's been here for 10 minutes! You're already driving her nuts."

I asked her if she'd like me to get off, she turned 16 shades of red – she was brand new to the class and she was dying inside - and she said, sheepishly, "Yes, please."

So first class with the new girl, I grab her pencil case and write "Donna loves Glen forever." This is the first time I've ever met her and I'm already driving her crazy. It's killing her. But it took three or four months of this relentless silliness, before she finally asked, "What will it take for you to stop bothering me?" And I said "Go on one date with me. Just one."

She looked at me and asked, "And then what?" And I said, "I promise I'll never bug you or phone you. Ever."

She said alright, we went on that date, true story, next day she doesn't call me.

So I waited until four o'clock and I phoned her, I said "It's Glen." and "You broke your rule, you said you wouldn't phone me."

"Obviously I lied. I need another date."

She went on one more date with me, she's been dating me ever since. We were 17 years old.

It is crazy but in a 10th Degree life we will talk about relationships, and there's a lot of material in there about being relentless and never giving up. I truly believe that if you make the decision to be with somebody and to love somebody, you're going to love that person forever. That's the way it is. I've proved it so far. I'm not suggesting that at 17 that is always the case, but as we mature and grow in our relationships, I absolutely believe that a decision has to be made about loving someone and never giving up on that love.

A PROPOSAL AND A WEDDING

One day Donna said to me, "the test is blue."

Of course, me being a dumb 19-year-old guy said, "What test?" and she said, "The test you get at the drugstore, Glen."

So there we are. We're both 19 years old and she's pregnant. I come from a background with no money to help or support me. I got a 19-year-old girl pregnant and there was never any question that I was going to marry her.

She told me in September and we were married in November 1991. I'm a husband and have to find a home and provide for a baby on the way. I really wanted to buy a house and things to put in the house. My mom as always reassured me and I was determined to do it on my own with no help from anyone.

I was able to do it at the start, partly because of the Manitoba tradition – the Wedding Social. I don't know anywhere else on the planet where people do it. The concept is frightfully simple. You set a date, rent a hall, sell tickets and have a big party. You sell raffle tickets and liquor and serve food and you raise money for the bride and groom. At the end of our social, we had enough money for a small down payment on a house.

Donna and I went out and bought our first house for $60,000 in rural Manitoba and we lived there while I refereed hockey, tended bar, sold cars off my driveway and worked on the floor at my uncle's car dealership. That's how I made ends meet.

Not surprisingly, our baby came quickly. We were married in November and the baby came in April. I had a $500 overdraft on my chequing account when Justin arrived. Believe me I had sleepless nights when the overdraft was maxed and I was 10 days away from the next payday.

Nobody gave us a chance on making it, but here we are, still here, together, 18 years later. That's love and that's Relationship Mastery, but we'll get to that later.

When Justin was born, money was tight and I was trying find ways to make ends meet.

The baby was colicky and allergic to breast milk and we had to put him on a special formula. He was the biggest kid ever. At six-months-old, he weighed more than my friend's two year old. Man this kid could eat, and he's costing me $300 a month in formula, because he's allergic to breast milk and I can't afford it. So what do I do? The only thing I knew how to do. Just like my mom taught me, I made it work.

I had a tab at the local store that I was running because everybody knew me in the small town and I've decided that I'm going to have to live the same life my mom did. Every pay cheque I would pay all my bills and I would be so excited if I was only down $100 in my bank account, because the way I saw it, I still had a $400 overdraft to get to the next pay period.

We had a house with no furniture in the living room except for a couch that Donna's father gave us. I went to the local Woolco Store and found some lamps that they were going to throw out because some kid had written on the lampshades (which I still have today, by the way) and I said, "Why are going to throw these out?" And the store clerk said, "There are chips on them." And I just asked, "Can I have them?" And the clerk said, "Sure you can have them."

So I took the lamps and went to the local liquor store and got two of those cool, thick wooden boxes the vineyards loaded with bottles of wine. Donna crocheted doilies to put over them and I colored them with a black marker and we put the doilies over them and put the free lamps on them. Those were our first end tables and lamps.

Donna's an extremely musical person and had completed the Grade 8 level for piano. She definitely wanted a piano of her own and it just so happened that a family friend of ours had a piano he didn't want and decided to sell it. Because I couldn't afford the piano, I made a deal with him. He allowed me a flexible repayment program, really flexible, and I can tell you this is another important example of relationships being a key to a 10th Degree life. Thank you John and Denise. We still have the piano today.

Meanwhile, it's our first anniversary and I promised myself that I would get a Donna a piano for her first anniversary. Man, this was going to be romantic.

At the local store where my sister used to work, I was able to charge a pizza (honest, for my first anniversary, I bought a pizza on credit). After picking up the pizza, I went down to the local liquor store and bought Baby Duck wine in a box. Wow! Was I romantic or what? Nothing but the best for Donna.

I had arranged to take Donna and Justin to my mom's place to be dropped off for a night with Grandma while my buddies moved the piano into the house.

When Donna, Justin and I arrived back at the house, we walked into the living room and there was this used piano sitting in the middle of the room. Donna started to cry. She looked at me and said, "I can't believe it!" So we sat on the floor, eating the pizza-purchased-on-credit and we had wine glasses that were given to us as a wedding gift, pouring Baby Duck from a box.

With our Baby Duck in our free wine glasses, we opened the box of pizza and ate on the floor and I looked at Donna and said, "Baby, it doesn't get any better than this."

Donna and I always said we would love to go on a cruise one day, so I asked her what she considered our first "big" anniversary. She thought about it for a second and said, "Our 10th Anniversary." So I told her I would take her on a cruise on the biggest ship anywhere she wanted to go on our 10th Anniversary and I would pay cash.

To this she replied, "Honey, I would be very happy with real end tables." Later in the book, in the section entitled, "Professional Mastery," I speak about goal setting. Unknowingly at the time, that's exactly what I did. I was determined to book that cruise for our anniversary, an anniversary that was still nine years away.

And I did book that cruise, on the biggest ship I could find. It was nine years later and, as promised, I paid cash. To this day, it is one of the warmest, one of the best feelings in my entire life.

FROM CHASING CHICKENS TO THE BIG OFFICE

I got into the car business when I worked for my dad for a few years at a little used car lot he started in Steinbach, a community of 8,000 just southeast of Winnipeg.

When that position became too stressful, I got a job selling new cars for a local Toyota dealer in Steinbach. I really thought I knew something about selling cars. But let me tell you, I quickly found out that I wasn't any better than the average sales person.

As a result, I wasn't making any real money and trying to provide for my wife and two young children was becoming very difficult. So I struggled for the first couple of months and then I had an epiphany.

I decided, "No, I'm not going to live my life this way. I am not going to struggle."

That's when I started to read about successful sales techniques. I read every book and every article I could get my hands on. I found people such as Grant Cardone, Joe Verde and Napoline Hill. I read everything I could from every important sales trainer out there and I started reading every word they wrote. I did start to get very, very serious.

I decided that in my professional mastery, I would do what every successful professional sales person would do. I started to practice all the things I had to do every day to turn my situation around. I learned to be very good on the phones. I learned professionalism and I learned to be very good with the public in the showroom. I sharpened everything – my greetings to people, my relationships with individuals – everything.

I came to the realization that in order to be successful, I had to be better than everybody, because I was in a commission-based environment and while I wanted to have friends, I was also in competition. Every day was a race for business and sales and I had to be the best.

I started to work very long hours to hone my craft. And to be honest, it didn't take long. In fact, it took about 90 days and I became the top sales person at that Toyota dealership and remained there for many months. I was 23 years old and I was finally making real money. I was making more money than anyone I knew at my age and I was really able to start putting some acorns in the tree for winter. At this stage, I knew I was really going to be able to provide for my family.

Meanwhile, as I became more successful, people in the business really started to take notice. I started to win awards and meet some really nice people, people I worked for, people in other businesses and to whom I sold automobiles. Before I knew it, all these offers started rolling in, but I just kept plugging away, learning more about the business and honing my craft until one day I got an offer to be a sales manager at another dealership. Then I got another one. Then another. Before I knew what was happening, I was juggling half a dozen offers.

But at one rural Ford dealership, the owner, Ron Delaquis, wanted me to not only come in and be the sales manager, but also teach the other sales people the secrets of my success – to teach them the methods that I used to sell the way I did.

Ron taught me almost everything I needed to know from the management side of things and while I was very successful on the sales side – and the success came quickly - Ron also gave me the opportunity to go out and do different things. I learned marketing, advertising and every aspect of the service department, all the while honing my sales skills.

And then he sent me to a leadership course in Philadelphia. My life changed in so many wonderful ways after that conference.

The most important thing I learned was about the importance of effective communication. You can't sell cars, you can't lead a group of sales people and you can't coach your employees, without effective communication skills. I learned a lot of great new skills at that conference but nothing was more important than the things I learned about communication. I also met a lot of very influential people and, honestly, it changed my life.

The conference introduced me to books that I'd never even seen let alone experienced and consumed. While there, I was introduced to the book that was probably the biggest influence in my life: *The Greatest Salesperson in the World* written by a brilliant author by the name of Og Mandino. Now Mandino has written some great books, and I've read them all, and every one them changed my life in some way, but there was nothing like *The Greatest Salesperson in the World*. It made my relationships stronger and my business acumen stronger. I have bought and given as gifts, more than 100 copies of that book.

I worked hard and got an offer to move to Winnipeg and work for a man who not only changed my life forever but influenced me more than any individual at any time in my business life - his name is Ashok Dilawri.

Ashok was a brilliant businessman who gave me the opportunity to take a little Acura dealership, one of his dealerships, that wasn't selling very many cars at all and he allowed me to put together a great team of hungry, dedicated young men, many of whom were already working there at the time, and make it a winner.

We started to inject all these different techniques and new styles of leadership, many of the concepts and processes that I learned in Philadelphia. We took all of the best information we had, put it into place and started a constant, continuous training program and quite frankly, it worked. We tripled our numbers.

As sales increased, my life caught on fire. I went from Sales Manger to General Manager and then I got promoted to General Manager at both the Toyota and the Acura stores, running two of the dealerships for Ashok's Dilawri Automotive Group.

Then I became Executive Vice President and Ashok and I went out and added other franchises to the group.

Eventually, Ashok named me President of the Dilawri Group and he kind of stepped back. I was now running all the operations for all of the car dealerships. The growth was amazing. I had a great team of people, people who were incredibly gifted, skilled and passionate.

We were probably one of the only automotive groups to do their own, consistent, three day-a-week training sessions for the in-house sales people. This was a group of automotive sales companies that did it all. I met some great people through the contacts I developed at the Dilawri Group. I started to feel again that it was time to continue the journey and leave the Dilawri automotive group. Ashok and his wife Annu were always terrific to Donna and I and we are still close to this day.

At this stage of my life, I was so interested in training sales people that training, not sales, was what I wanted to do for the rest of my life. After I left the automotive group I hit the road: Training at a few different places and speaking to a number of groups across Canada. I loved it. But there was one problem. And in the end, it turned out to be a pretty big problem: I missed my wife and I missed my kids.

I loved training and speaking to corporate and non-corporate groups on the road, especially as I developed the concept of the 10th Degree. In fact, it was almost completely set up at this stage, honed and ready to take to the world. But I have to admit, I wasn't ready for the travel with two boys at home who were just so much fun to be around.

I had to make a decision and, in the end, the decision was quite simple. I got together with my uncle, Chris Daman, and he offered me an opportunity to join him in his Winnipeg Hyundai dealership.

Chris not only offered to let me join him as the General Manger and as a partner which allows me to enjoy the best of all my worlds: I can write a book that will tell people all over the planet about the beauty of living a 10th Degree life, I get to speak on the road when I want to go, I get to spend all the time I possibly can with my family, I still get to meet new people, and I have now started life coaching, an experience that has been truly amazing.

"Every day, we aspire to inspire."

- **Scott Taylor**

I love the feeling I get from elevating the person across from me. We'll talk later in the book about "Relationship Mastery." It is not only important with our close inner circle of friends and family but, in fact, it's important to consider with everyone we touch.

The 10th Degree relationship mastery means leaving everyone around you feeling happy, comfortable and uplifted. It either reinforces their positive attitude and enthusiasm or it gives them hope when they feel there is none and confidence when they need it. Whether that interaction is with a co-worker dissatisfied with his job, friend having trouble at home, a classmate being bullied, a stranger you sit beside in the airport, a person with special needs or a player you coach, your ability to elevate the people around you can never be considered unimportant. I believe that even if you're just filling in as a shoulder to cry on, at a time when someone needs it, every encounter you have with another man, woman or child is another opportunity to make a difference in someone's life.

I believe that if each of us strives to reach a 10th Degree Relationship Mastery with every person we touch we can change the thinking, actions and overall attitude of entire communities, our nation and ultimately the world. And we can accomplish that one interaction at a time.

If I get a person to the next level of his or her life, and see them take that step, it's a greater payment than money. I really believe that my reason for existence on this planet is to help people go from one level to the next. And this book will take more people than I can get to, one-on-one, to the next – to the highest – level of their lives.

So come on in, read this book and join me on the journey. Let me guide you to the 10th Degree.

GETTING ALL GEEKED UP

"Play your music loud, Dance like no one is watching
and dream large!"

- Glen Daman

THE GLEN DAMAN PRESENTATION

"In the race for success, there is no finish line."
- Michael G. Winston

If you've seen them live, Glen Daman's training sessions and the 10th Degree presentations leave participants with one feeling: "When can we do this again?"

He is dynamic, funny, and, of course, he comes right at you with enthusiasm and the very best attitude in the entire world.

Glen's basic premise, from the day the 10th Degree was honed, was this: "How do we make a bigger impact on the people we care about?" His message is powerful and it has a positive effect on both our personal and professional lives.

So now that you have picked up this booked and read this far, you are ready for the overview. Open your mind and let this information in. It's not New Age; it's not directed at one religious group or another. It's a practical approach to life and much of it, you've heard before.

However, if you buy in, if you "Drink the Kool-Aid" as they say, you will have a better life. That's a guarantee.

You are about to get a little taste of the 10th Degree. A pre-synopsis, if you will. It's from one of Glen's many presentations and it's told in a way that's relevant to the every day life of almost everyone living in the industrialized world.

This is your first step. If you like what you what you hear, Glen will take you much deeper. But first, you need to get "Geeked Up."

- Scott Taylor

GETTING GEEKED UP: AN OVERVIEW
HOW TO GET READY TO START YOUR DAY

"I don't have time to take care of myself is like saying, I don't have time to stop and buy gas because I'm driving too fast."
- Robin Sharma

"Who's All Geeked Up??!!"
"Are you All Geeked Up!!!?? Are you??!!"
Let's hear it! I'm All Geeked Up!!"

I love that. I love to be excited about everything I do. So here's the deal: What I'm going to tell you wasn't thought up over dinner one evening. It came from discussions and presentations that I've had with people and done with people over a number of years. This program was built, not invented.

And I'll tell you this: I love to live this stuff the best I can. I'm All Geeked Up all the time. And if I can pass this on to you, you will live a better life. There is no doubt about that.

What if I told you that if you take the things I'm going to talk about and used them every day, it would change your life for the better, would you accept my challenge? Yes or no?

Yes? Good.

And if you could take yourself from a level way down here and move it way up here, would you do it? Yes or no? I want to take everyone reading this to a place where they've never gone before but I must caution you, I'll get you there, it's up to you to stay there.

If I said to you, 'Give me 60 minutes of your day, every day and I will double your income,' will you do it? Yeah, you will. What if I said that if you give me 60 minutes a day and by doing that you could reach all of your physical goals, strengthen your relationships and improve your outlook on life? Would you do it? Yes or no? If the answer is yes, then read on.

So who's busy? We're all busy. If you're busy it's hard to give up 60 minutes of your day, but if I said, give me 60 minutes of your day every day and I guaranteed it would give you a better life, would you follow my advice? Yes or no?

Well then, I want one hour of your day before you normally get up. In other words, if you get up at 7 a.m., you'll now get up at 6. If you're a shift-worker and you normally get up at 9 p.m., you're now going to get up at 8 p.m. I want that hour. Just 60 minutes. And I want it one hour before you get out of bed now. That's because I want you doing this stuff before you do anything else.

Now I'll admit, it's tough to get out of bed in the morning, isn't it? Well, it's not if you have something to live for.

When you start your day, there is a difference between showing up and stepping up. I want you to show up AND step up every single day. To do that, you have to get started first thing in the morning.

So here's Step 1: Physical Mastery. Every single day.

I'm not asking you to lose weight. I'm not asking you to gain weight. I'm asking you to get physically prepared every single day and here's how it works.

I'll start with this question: Does energy sell? Of course, it sells. If you have energy, you can sell a whole lot better than the guy who isn't physically ready for his day. And if you say to me, "I don't care, I'm not in sales," my response will be, "Bummer, sucks to be you."

Just kidding. It doesn't matter if you're in sales or not. That's because we are ALWAYS selling. You're always selling yourself and if you have more energy, would that help you sell you? If you were geeked up to a higher level of energy than everyone else, would that help or hinder your ability to sell you? I suspect it would help, wouldn't it?

So we agree physical prep is important, but what do we do every morning for our physical preparation for the day? I don't care. Just get your blood flowing. What does blood carry? That's right, oxygen. And what is oxygen good for?

Thinking? Somebody said, "thinking." That's a good one. It's right, too. But not only does it help you think, it gets every other part of your body ready to go to work, too – whatever that work might be. To get all geeked up, you need oxygen to get all geeked up.

So I want you to give me 20 minutes every single day. I want that 20 minutes in the morning. I want you to dance across your living room like Tom Cruise in his underwear in that old movie. Or, heck, you can do jumping jacks, push ups, run around your block, ride your exercise bike, run up and down your stairs. I don't care what you do. You don't need to join a gym to do this – although it would be great if you did – you just need to do something physical first thing every morning. (If you saw the movie Invictus, you saw that the great Nelson Mandela, when he was in his mid-70s and was President of South Africa, started every day with a long walk around his neighborhood. This is simple.)

I don't care what you do, but for 20 minutes first thing every day, I want you to be active. There, that's your workout program. That's it. How would you like me to be your personal trainer?

"What do you want me to do, Glen?"
"Run."

"But I don't like to run."

"OK then, fall down and get up and fall down and get up and do it for 20 minutes and there, you're done."

Wouldn't you love me to be your personal trainer? I don't care what you do. Do something! Anything. Perfect. We get RESULTS here, don't we!

So now, you usually get up at 7 a.m., but now you'll get up at 6 and you'll do 20 minutes worth of sit-ups or you'll run or you'll walk. Do you think you will feel different?

Of course you will. It's 20 minutes later and you've done something physical. Of course, you'll feel different. You'll feel a lot better, too.

Ultimately, we want to dance, run, walk, whatever it is, in order to create an energized environment. Because if you have an energized environment what does that mean for everyone around you?

It gives you, me, everyone positivity! That's what you have. Negativity is contagious. It poisons everything. But positivity is contagious and it results from an energized environment.

Of course, people will think you're whacked when you're happy and positive all the time:

Tom: "What's wrong with that guy?"
Dick: "Don't know, he's always like that."
Tom: "Can't be."
Dick: "Oh he is."
Tom: "On drugs, obviously."
Dick: "Nope, he's just positive all the time."

They might think you're completely whacked, but you're not.

You just have the energy they don't have.

Attitude. 88 per cent of success or lack of success is predicated by your attitude. Now, not everybody in this room has a great attitude. Can everyone here admit that they could take it up a notch or two? Yes? Well, consider these premises:

"Success is achieved faster and more easily with a positive attitude."

"You'll have more happiness in your life with a positive attitude."

Stop me if you disagree!

"If you have a positive attitude, you have more energy. If you have more energy, you have greater inner power and strength."

"A positive attitude gives you the ability to inspire yourself and others."

Do we agree with all of that? Absolutely.

Now, don't forget this. What we're talking about is selfish. You have to look after your attitude. You have to take care of yourself before you can take care of everyone around you. Ever wonder why that flight attendant says, "Make sure to put on your oxygen mask before helping others around you, even small children?" It's because if you aren't conscious, how can you help those around you? You must first make sure you are able to do the things that need to be done

before you can help those around you. Same goes for attitude. If you have a bad attitude, everybody around you has a bad attitude. Remember, like the flu, attitude, good or bad, is contagious.

We work on ourselves first. You have to have your attitude in the right place before you can take others with you.

Here's another one: "With a positive attitude, fewer difficulties will be encountered along the way." Agree? Absolutely!

A positive attitude will result in fewer problems in your life. Does that not mean that with a bad attitude, you'll encounter more difficulties. Yes, it does. Could most of the difficulties we face in life be caused by us? Yep. I call it the mirror test. My wife thinks I have all these mirrors in our house because I'm vain and because I'm so handsome and I have to keep looking at myself, but that's only partly true. There are mirrors all over the place so I'll know who to blame when I have a bad attitude. That's the truth.

Here's one: "Life smiles at you." Remember that.

How will you develop a positive attitude that will lead to success? Well, you have to choose. You have to choose to be happy. You get up every morning and you have to choose to have a positive attitude. You have to choose to have faith in yourself and in the power of the universe. You have to choose to associate with the right, positive, happy people.

We choose the people we have around us. Attitude is the same thing. If you want to take your attitude to a new level, you have to do one of two things with the people around you: You have to be sure they're adding, not subtracting, but adding to your attitude or you have to be selfish. It's simple. Do we know people who only want to talk about the car crash, the break-in, the fire, the guy that died, the people who just split up? Do we? You know 'em. They can't wait to run up to you and tell you all the bad stuff. Well, that's a sign.

Run the other way!

You understand. You get it. Choose to have a good attitude.

So now we can move on to Step 2: Mental Mastery

Mental Mastery. How do you get to mental mastery? Can you actually work on attitude? Absolutely! People believe you either have a good attitude or you don't. I say, "No, you can work on having a good attitude."

We've worked out for 20 minutes, now, for the next minutes we're going to work on our attitude. And we're going to do that by reading. That's right. I want you to read.

OK, I know some of you will say, "Ah, but I don't like to read." And, I say,

"Bummer, get over it." You have to read!

But you have to be very careful. I don't want you to read just anything. I want you to read 15 minutes a day. All positive stuff.

My grandma used to say: "Garbage in, garbage out." How about positive in, positive out? Nobody ever thinks of that. Many think they have to stop reading because all they read is garbage. Negative garbage. Wrong. There is a lot of positive stuff out there to read. I mean it, there are so many great authors: Robin Sharma, Ken Blanchard, Mike Lipkin, the Dalai Lama, Og Mandino. The list is long. Go to the bookstore and find them. Read them. Or, if you're lazy, just Google, "Inspiration" and your computer will explode with available information. There is all kinds of great stuff.

So tell me this: If you just completed Step 1 and Step 2, would you be a better person tomorrow? Yes, you would. Your thinking creates your reality. Don't ever forget that. Pump it into you. Be positive. 15 minutes a day.

I once heard a speaker ask his audience this: "Did you know that 90 per cent of million dollar homes have a library in them?"

Coincidence? I think not. But here's an even cooler stat. "100 per cent of those people in the million dollar homes had the books before they built the house." That's part of the reason they got there.

Success isn't necessarily measured by money. We just all react to money as being the measure of success. But the most successful people in the world don't ever talk about money. They talk about what they did and whom they did it with. Every successful person I know talks about the wonderful positive things they read every single day.

If we cut out the negativity when we read, it really makes a huge difference in our attitude.

Do you read the newspaper? Stop! What sells newspapers? Positivity or negativity? That's right, negativity. Bad things. Don't read the newspaper. I mean, is there anything in the newspaper we desperately have to read?

Your horoscope? Sure. The comics are OK. The crossword. Absolutely. I read the sports page but even that is becoming too negative for me.

Someone once said to me, "Well, it's good to read the newspaper to find out who died?" Really? If the person who just died was close to you, you'd know long before it's in the paper.

"Oh look, mom's dead. It's right here in the paper." I think if mom died, you'd probably be the first to know.

There's nothing in a newspaper that helps you. Nothing in a newspaper helps give you a good attitude. Stop reading it.

And here's an interesting stat. Canadians watched an average of 7 ½ hours of TV per day. Per day! Are you kidding? That's more than 50 hours a week.

OK, is it positive or negative on TV? Most of it is negative. CNN, CBC News, CTV News – all negative. Even weather is always negative. I mean have you watched the weather? "There is a 60 per cent chance of rain." It's never a 40 per cent chance of sunshine. Ever! That's because negative, hurtful, bad, it all sells.

Even the show *Survivor* is all about the negative. We aren't voting who to keep on the island. We're voting to kick someone off.

Negative, negative, negative. And negative obviously makes people rich. So true. So sad.

Think about you're TV viewing. Every day. Stay away from newspapers and TV news. Nothing good can come of it. Never forget, positive in, positive out.

So what do we have now? We have 20 minutes of physical prep, 15 minutes of mental prep. That's 35 minutes. We're feeling pretty good right now, aren't we?

Let's go on to Step 3: We have to get ready emotionally. This is Emotional Mastery.

Do we have problems in our life? Yes or no? Of course, we do. But think about our "Circle of Life."

This represents everything that's good in our life. Then we have the girlfriend or wife problem.

And we have problem at work.

And our transmission's busted.

This is all stressing us out, making us miserable. Ruining our great attitude. Tearing down our lives.

So what do we see now? We see a big white circle with three little black dots. There is a heck of a lot more white space than black isn't there? One problem though. We just can't take our eyes off the dots. We always look at the black dots and ignore the huge white space.

In order to become emotionally strong, we must learn to concentrate on the white space. Look, I have a wonderful wife, two beautiful sons, a great home life, a great career, plenty of friends I love and no matter what else is going on in my life, that's what I concentrate on. That's my big white space. Do I have problems? Of

course, I do. But those problems can't consume my life because I know that even though I have black dots, I have more white space.

If we do this for five minutes every day when we get up, if we just sit down after our workout and our read and we concentrate on the white space – the wonderful things in our life – and just focus on all the good that is around us, don't you think it would make a difference? Don't you think it would give us a better attitude and prepare us to face our day with confidence and a feeling that life is truly wonderful. Of course, it would.

The little dots aren't very big are they? If you get up and deal with them, they will – I guarantee it – fade away. Start your day with a great attitude and a resolve to do the very best you can to make the little dots fade away. Make the circle completely blank. But start by spending five minutes every morning focusing on the good things in that big white space.

That will get you to Emotional Mastery. That's called focusing on the positive. Let's move on.

Step 4: It's time to get energy ready. How do we do that? Breakfast, of course!

So how do we eat? Does that sound like dumb question? How do we eat? There are no dumb questions. Most people don't have any idea how to eat. Should we have Tim Hortons? No? Starbucks? No? You're right. That's not breakfast. Now, don't get me wrong I love going to those places and I do. However, the morning must start with a well balanced breakfast. We need juice and oatmeal. We need some protein, some eggs and we need carbs, we need toast.

Whatever you happen to enjoy in the morning – that isn't a donut or a cheese Danish – you should have every morning. Some fruit? A banana? You need to eat the things that will jump start your metabolism. You have to be putting real fuel into your body (later we'll introduce you to the Canada Food Guide).

Think about it. Are you getting tired and hungry at 10 a.m.? Then again at 3 p.m.? Is that happening to you? You're not getting enough of the good stuff in the morning after your workout. You're burning it up. If that's happening, bring some snacks to work. And I'm not talking about candy or taco chips. Bring healthy fuel – fruit, yogurt, carrots and celery – to help you keep the gas tank full all day.

Do you think you'd feel healthier if you did that? Absolutely! And if we felt healthier every day, what do you think that would do for your attitude? Automatically, it would make your attitude even more positive. What would that do for your energy level and your success in life? I believe it would skyrocket, wouldn't it?

"Hey, who wants to go on a rocket!!!??" "Who's All Geeked Up!!!??"

We're energy ready. You just need 10 minutes to sit down and eat a nutritious breakfast. We're energy prepped for the day. Just 10 minutes. That's all it takes.

Now, on to Step 5: Professional Mastery.

What do you know about goals? How many of you have set specific, clear, written goals?

Not a very high percentage set goals but don't beat yourself up. That's not surprising at all, it's the norm.

While most of us seldom even bother to set goals, let alone write them down, I have to tell you there are few things in life that are more important.

Experts and authors in sales and professional success, people who came along before me, have all agreed that goal setting is an important aspect of the visual creation of your ideal future. We've talked about visualization. Well, the only way to visualize your future is to think about it, decide where you want to be and what you want to be doing and take the right steps to get there. You do that by sitting down, setting clear and specific goals and then writing them down on a piece of paper so you can go back and refer to them tomorrow and the next day and the next day.

By writing down your goals and referring to them often, you can motivate yourself to turn your personal vision of a perfect future into reality.

We all have goals of some kind, but by writing down your goals, it suddenly makes them more real. It gives you the opportunity to pull out your notes at any time, look at them and study them. More importantly, it holds you accountable to yourself.

It's also important to understand that if you set goals and you write them down, it can be quite motivating. That's your future. In a few simple words, written on a piece of paper that only you can see. As well, when you reach your goals – and if you live the 10th Degree, you will reach your goals – you'll find that you will also build your self-confidence. You will now know that you can go to the places you want to reach and you even have written proof that you've made it.

So No. 5 is a simple 10 minute assignment. Focus on our goals. I call that being professionally prepped.

You have 10 minutes every day – not to write down our goals but to look at your goals and focus on them, to review them and make sure you are on target.

It will take you a lot longer to write down your goals so don't do that first thing in the morning. Take a weekend and write down your goals. What I want from you is to take 10 minutes at the start of your day to focus on and review those goals.

Wait a minute. Do we only have professional goals? Don't we have other goals? Don't we have relationship goals? Weight-loss or weight-gain goals? If there is something, anything in your life you want to improve on, you should sit at a table, set a goal and write it down.

Here's a tip. If you set a goal, put a timeline on it. Write down the amount of time you want to take to reach your goal(s) and review it everyday. Refer to it often. Study it. Ask yourself, "Am I getting close?" You want to lose 20 pounds? So how long do you want to take to lose 20 pounds? Six months? One year? So if you say one year, how many pounds do you want to lose in six months? 10, right? Put a timeline on it.

If you do that, you can work it backwards and put a daily goal on it. And if you look at it every day for 10 minutes, you'll know exactly where you are. You'll know exactly when to step on the gas or take it off.

What's the first thing you do when you want to go someplace, but you have no idea how to get there. You look at a map, right? Why don't we do that with our lives?

I have a clear, specific written goal. How am I going to get there? I don't know. I guess I'll just hope. Really? True, the blind squirrel does find an acorn from time to time, I get that. But without a written plan with a timeline, you're going to have to do a lot of hoping. Oh yeah, and you are not a blind squirrel.

Remember, time will come to an end. No goal will be reached. You absolutely MUST have a clear, specific, written goal with a timeline or you're going to go nowhere. And then you have to take

10 minutes every day to review it. Just to make sure you're exactly where you should be.

OK, let's review...

1. Physical Mastery – 20 minutes
2. Mental Mastery – 15 minutes
3. Emotional Mastery -- 5 minutes
4. Fueled up – 10 minutes
5. Professional Mastery -- Goal review – 10 minutes

That's it! You're ready to start. You're ready to go to work, or go to school or take care of your kids.

If we took one hour every day – at the start of each day – and did all we've discussed, would we be better off? Absolutely! Would you be All Geeked Up!!!! Of course, you would.

You deserve to be happy. You deserve to be a success. Do all of the steps every day – for just one hour at the start of your day -- and you will be happy and successful. Later in the book we will discuss the final cornerstone, mastery if you will, to a 10th Degree life -   Relationship Mastery.

OK, let me ask you this: If you did all of the points in the 60 minutes allotted, how do you think you would you feel? Great? Physically? Great? Mentally? Great? Finally, how would your attitude be? Tremendous? How do you think this would affect your relationships? Pretty cool right?

You're ready. Let's start our journey toward living a successful 10th Degree life.

Five Quick Tips to Living a 10ᵗʰ Degree Life

1. Exercise every morning, this jump starts your metabolism and gets your blood moving. What does blood carry? Oxygen. What does oxygen give you? Energy for the entire day and you always want to start early in the morning.

2. Start each day with a game plan and focus on it. Not, "Oh let's see what happens," but a real plan. If I was going to drive to the store six blocks away, I would automatically have a plan on how to get to that store. We don't get in the car and "just see what happens." If we did that, we'd never get the bread.

3. Read something inspirational and motivational every single day. If you want to have a positive, successful life, you need to get jacked up. Get geeked up! People ask me everyday, "What are you on, man?" My answer is simple: "I'm on motivation. I'm on inspiration." Every single day.

4. Eat right. If your body is your vehicle for life, which I believe it is, then the food we put in it is the fuel. It's real simple; it's just like a car - the higher the grade of gasoline, the better the performance. Well, we're just like a car. You go to that store and the higher the octane value in that fuel, the better your body's going to perform. Simple.

5. And this is an all-time Glen Daman favourite: Before we close our eyes each night, before you put your head down on that pillow, I want every single person to finish this sentence "The best thing about today was _____" and you fill in the blank. And it has to be a positive thing, it can't be "The best thing of today was me going to sleep to forget it." No, there has to be something we did or talked about or thought about that was amazing today. This will help you fall asleep every night with a smile. And falling asleep with a smile,

to me, is an extremely important step toward living a 10th Degree
life.

ORDINARY MIRACLES

"Today I wish you a day of ordinary miracles ~ A fresh pot of coffee you didn't make yourself. An unexpected phone call from an old friend. Green stoplights on your way to work. The fastest line at the grocery store. A good sing-along song on the radio. Your keys found right where you left them."

- Unknown

LIVING THE 10TH DEGREE

"You don't have to be successful or wealthy to get started on a 10th Degree Life. But you do have to get started to reach the 10th Degree."

- Glen Daman

ONE WORD: ATTITUDE

"Our thoughts are the steering wheel to our actions. What we do affects not only today, but tomorrow. Our thoughts are driven by our attitude. That is the main ingredient. In the 10th Degree life, attitude is a decision. We decide what we watch, what we read, what words we speak and who we include in our circle of influence. We choose our attitude and it influences our thoughts, thus steering us on the road to success and a10th Degree life."

- Glen Daman

Some people are more talented than others and some are more educated. Some simply have more privileges. Some are born with a silver spoon in their mouths and are given a better start at life than the vast majority of us. Doesn't matter. Everyone has the ability to be great. You are limited only by your imagination, determination, resilience, the choices you make and most of all, ATTITUDE.

If you attack every day feeling good about yourself, smiling, making the people around you better, then you have taken the first, important step to living a 10th Degree life.

You can't make a positive impression on the people around you, the people you need to impress the first time, without having a positive attitude. How do we get a positive attitude? We choose it.

That's right, it's simple: Attitude is a choice. In fact, our entire life is one big choice. We can choose to take it on with a smile and a kind word or we can choose to be angry and hurtful.

I will talk, when we get to Professional Mastery, about the choice you have every morning before you go to work or school. In fact, when I speak to corporate groups or sales teams, I always ask them: Which guy do you want to be?

Do you want to be this guy? "Oh, it's raining. The weather's lousy. It's awful/ Nobody will leave home today. We're not going to have any business at all, there's no water in the water cooler. Nobody ever cares about us or even the damn water cooler. This place is a dump. I hate it here. I don't know about you, but if there was a better job, I'd be gone. I'd go get it. I'd be out of here."

Does that sound familiar? Sure, in millions and millions of offices all over the world, there are angry people speaking every language known to man moaning and groaning and whining and crying all the time. Nothing but anger and self-pity and negativity all the time.

Well, let me be brutally honest: I don't want to hang with that guy. Do you? Do you want that negativity nattering in your ear all day? Didn't think so.

I'd rather hang around with this guy: "Morning boys, what's up this morning? Did you see that football game last night? Wow! That was an offensive battle wasn't it? Are you kidding me? Unbelievable. I notice there's no water in the water cooler, but until the guy comes in to replace the bottle, I brought a couple of bottles of water from home. They're in the fridge, help yourself. What's going on folks? Anything you need? Anything I can get anybody? Are you all ready to be successful today?"

So tell me, which guy would you rather work with? The guy who is happy, ready to get it on, ready to help, ready to make you happy or the guy who hates everything, especially you, and spends the morning whining, not working.

Now look, I'm not naïve. I know there are all sorts of people who just feed off the negativity. But if everyone got on the 10th Degree program, what a wonderful world this would be.

When I think about attitude it reminds me of one of my favourite quotes. It's from a Texas-based Evangelical Pastor named Charles R. Swindoll. Now, I don't base anything I do on any particular Christian, Muslim or even Buddhist teaching. I certainly believe in spirituality, but I'm also a pragmatist. We all have things we need to do in our lives that make us feel good, or comfortable or safe. I'll let people like Swindoll deal with that. What I want for you is to be happy, healthy and make the right choices, the choices that make people around you feel good about you and themselves.

There is nothing that makes me happier than when I can lift up the person standing in front of me. That's why I love Swindoll's quote:

"The longer I live, the more I realize the impact of attitude on life. Attitude, to me, is more important than facts. It is more important that the past, the education, the money, than circumstances, than failure than successes, than what other people think or say or do. It is more important than appearance, giftedness or skill. It will make or break a company... a church... a home. The remarkable thing is we have a choice everyday regarding the attitude we will embrace for that day. We cannot change our past... we cannot change the fact that people will act in a certain way. We cannot change the inevitable. The only thing we can do is play on the one string we have, and that is our attitude. I am convinced that life is 10 per cent what happens to me and 90 per cent of how I react to it. And so it is with you... we are in charge of our attitudes."

In psychology, attitude is defined as: "... a hypothetical construct that represents an individual's degree of like or dislike for an item. Attitudes are generally positive or negative views of a person, place, thing, or event-- this is often referred to as the attitude object. People can also be conflicted or ambivalent toward an object, meaning that they simultaneously possess both positive and negative attitudes toward the item in question."

That's certainly scientific, but for you and me, and everyone around us, attitude is the most important choice we make every day. If you take a happy, positive, friendly, helpful, empathetic attitiude with you every day, it will make your life and the lives of the people with whom you come in contact with better. And isn't that, ultimately, what we all want to do?

ATTITUDE IN REACTION

Now, it's one thing to walk out the door every day and convince yourself that you're going to have a great attitude that day. That's a good choice, but things happen during a day that can play havoc with your positive approach to life.

In fact, it's a real challenge keeping a great attitude for an entire day.

Things happen that can really ruin your outlook on life.

With that in mind, I want to remind you of what the great writer Robin Sharma, once said: "It's not what happens to us that matters, but how we react to what happens to us."

As you've read, I will always encourage you to focus on the positives and choose a great attitude every morning: If not for you, for your friends, family and co-workers. Ultimately, your family, your health and your friends depend on it.

When you really stop and think about it, having a negative attitude is one of the most selfish acts there is. We affect so many people, every day, within our inner circle of influence that the last thing we want to do is make them miserable. For most of us, this inner circle is made up of the people we love and respect, so why would we approach them with anything but our best possible outlook on life – a positive attitude?

As we get further toward the 10th Degree, we will talk about Emotional Mastery. A major element in mastering our emotions is the ability to take a step back.

No matter what happens, during the day: If someone offends you, if they negatively criticize your work, if they ask you to do something you'd rather not, something that is immoral or you simply don't feel right doing, whenever anything like that happens, do what

I call "take a step back."

It never hurts to just take a breath before responding to a situation. Most of what happens to you in your life is a result of how you respond to external stimuli. And what people do TO you is much more difficult to handle properly than what people do FOR you.

In those stressful situations, the ones in which you would like to say something that you know will hurt you in the morning, just take a deep breath, a step back and as my mother used to say, "Count to 10." I would argue back then, that after a minute or two, I still felt the same way and she'd respond by saying: "Keep counting!"

I've never forgotten those words and they've served me well. I can also tell you this -- from experience: More often than not, when I react too quickly to a difficult situation, I end up feeling sorry for the words I use, and unfortunately once you've said something hurtful, you really can't take it back. When I utter angry words that I regret, it leaves me feeling less than the 10th Degree.

So remember, start your day with a great attitude and do you're very best to keep that attitude all day long, despite the problems you might face. Think positively and always be prepared to take a step back.

"Things will go wrong at times in life. We can't control everything that happens to us. We can however choose how we react. We choose what we do after things happen. We choose our attitude. Life is a series of choices and we control our own lives with them."

- Glen Daman

IS YOUR GLASS HALF-FULL OR HALF-EMPTY?

"You can complain because roses have thorns, or you can rejoice

because thorns have roses."

- Ziggy Marley

Are you generally a positive person? Are you what we call a "glass-half-full" kind of person?

Or are you usually negative? Do things that happen around you always get you down? Do you hate the boss? Don't like your co-workers? Are you a glass-half-empty type of person?

As we discussed in Attitude in Reaction, we all experience bad things. Ups and downs come and go every single day. And as you already know, how we deal with what happens to us every day is what is most important.

If you start the day with a negative attitude you are bound for failure. It's like a self-fulfilling prophecy. If you think you will fail, you will fail. If you think you will be successful, chances are in your favour that you will be successful. Just like one of the most successful business people of all time, Henry Ford, said: "Whether you think you can or can't, your right."

Think of the happiest, most successful person you have ever met and ask yourself this: How did he/she get so successful? There is one thing I can guarantee. He did not become successful and happy by taking every failure and saying, "That's it! It quit!" I can't do this. I'm done! This will never work! This doesn't have a chance! I'm a failure, I give up!" That person never got successful by letting negativity control his/her life.

I absolutely guarantee that even when a project fails, successful people do not quit. They gather up their glass-half-full attitude and get back to work.

It's been said: "The satisfaction and happiness you derive from life depends on your dreams, goals, attitude and actions. Those who wait for life to supply satisfaction and happiness usually end up with heartache and sorrow instead."

When I was young, I learned something from my mom that was extremely important to me. Although I'm not sure she ever said it to me in so many words, her actions always demonstrated this: "There is no such word as can't." As you'll soon learn, my mom did everything she possibly could, all by herself, to give me, my brother and my sister a great childhood filled with love and caring -- even when there wasn't much money. She never said, "can't," and always found a way.

Consider looking into the mirror in the morning and saying this to yourself: "If I get up every morning and start my day with a positive attitude, I have the most important tool I need to be successful in anything I desire."

That's a glass-half-full approach to your day. Anything positive is always better than anything negative.

Here are some tips to start your day, every day, with a positive attitude. This is how to keep our glass half-full.

1. I will always take responsibility for my own actions.

2. I will never blame others for my failures. Instead I will learn from those failures and I will try again. I will never quit.

3. I will be aware of my thoughts at all times. I will concentrate on my own power to overcome any and all negative thoughts. If I start my day by reading positive, powerful, uplifting words, I will get off to a great start and I will maintain that attitude from the start of my day until I go to bed each night.

4. I will never focus on what's missing in my life. I will always take a few moments at various times each day to count my blessings and think about all the positive things I have in my life.

5. When things don't go my way, I will take a step back. I will "Count to 10." I will consider my words carefully. I will not react to the negative, but in time I will respond.

6. Never forget, life is a series of choices and we can control our choices. We can choose to be positive or choose to be negative. Nothing good ever comes from negative.

VISUALIZATION

Here's something you've probably heard before: If you can visualize it, you can do it. In fact, it's been said that as soon as you completely understand that you have no limits to what you can accomplish – and then, by letting your imagination soar -- everything is possible to you.

Professional golfers will all tell you that as part of their pre-shot ritual, they always visualize where the ball will land. They see it and then they do it. The same goes for all of us, especially when we aren't playing golf.

One way to start your day as positively as possible is to believe in yourself. As we get closer to the 10th Degree, you will start to believe in your abilities and skills more and more each day. As you gain Physical Mastery, Mental Mastery and Emotional Mastery, you will begin to understand that you are in control, not your boss, or your boyfriend or your peer group. You!

However, to guarantee that you get through those steps, you must have a positive attitude. And when I say, "You can do it!" I mean it. I did it and I started in a trailer on the edge of a farmer's field.

To succeed in any area of your life, whether it's in your personal relationships, in how you feel about yourself or how you handle the things that come your way at work, you must start with a positive attitude.

We have heard so many times that "Life is what you make it." And that's absolutely true. You can visualize a life for yourself that is steeped in happiness, wrapped in great relationships and packaged up with all sorts of business, artistic or personal successes. In fact, many people believe in creating Vision Boards so they can more easily visualize their goals. To them, I say, "Bravo!"

In the meantime, you can visualize a life that's full of anger, revenge, ugliness and hatred. Remember, it's your choice and this I can guarantee: If you are negative, if negativity controls your life, you will be pulled down into the depths of despair. But if you are positive, happy and uplifting, then your success knows no bounds. You can be whatever you want to be. And you can be happy while you work hard to reach your dreams.

Which attitude will you chose?

"Life is broken down to the second. We must savor every one of them. It's been said we only live once so live life to its fullest. Life has no practice rounds, no dress rehearsals. Live now, love now with no fear."

- Glen Daman

Remember: We all choose our attitude. It's as simple as that.

LIVE IN THE MOMENT

"If you are still talking about what you did yesterday, you haven't done much today."

- Unknown

One of the truly negative emotions that can destroy a good attitude is worry. Worry about something that happened in the past or, worse, worry about something that might happen in the future. There is really nothing sillier than that. You might think you know what's going to happen, but really you do not have a clue.

So quit worrying. Start living.

Here are a handful of things we'll be discussing in the pages of this book. Each one of these items will give you a meaningful way to live each day "in the moment":

1. Get up every morning, exercise, have a great breakfast, read something uplifting and choose to have a great attitude before you head off to start your day.

2. Surround yourself with people who make you feel good, people who are as positive as you are. There is no room for negativity in a 10th Degree life. The only way to live in the moment is to be happy with the moment.

3. Visualize the life you want and never lose that visualization. You can have the life you want if your glass is half full and your attitude is positive.

4. Laugh out loud and do it every chance you get. Live every moment as richly as you can.

5. Be thankful for all the great things you have in your life and when you find yourself in a potentially negative situation, think about all of those things you have that are truly, truly wonderful.

6. Imagine it's the last time you'll ever experience whatever you're experiencing at this moment. To truly live in the moment, you need to slow down and savor the present. If you knew that the moment you were currently living in would create a powerful memory, would you savor it more?

7. When you wake up, smile. It's going to be another great day.

8. Commit random acts of kindness, even if it's just a kind word. If it makes the people around you better, you have made the world a better place in that moment. Remember: You can never be sensitive to other people's needs if you don't know their needs at that moment. Remember, always give more than you take.

9. Be thankful for what you have, not what you don't have. Be thankful for the moment you are living in right now, not a moment tomorrow or a moment last week.

10. Finally, here is something that I will refer to again – more than once: Life is broken down to the second. Savor everyone of those seconds. It has been said that we only live once, so live life to its fullest. Life has no practice rounds, no dress rehearsals. So live now for the moment you're in.

WHY WOULDN'T YOU?

Before we embark on our five-step journey toward the 10th Degree, I want to share with you, something that I just love.

When people come up to me and ask me something crazy, something like, "Glen, I've been asked by a friend to go dog-sledding in Alaska. What do you think?"

Those kinds of questions always make me smile. When something is physically positive, mentally positive and emotionally positive, I almost always say the same thing: "Why wouldn't ya?"

Why wouldn't ya? I love it.

Whenever an opportunity comes up in your life – and it might be the craziest thing you could ever imagine – if it doesn't hurt you or your family, if it isn't illegal or immoral and it doesn't injure another person, why wouldn't you try it?

Consider this: If and when some crazy opportunity makes itself available to you, don't say yes or no that second. Step back and think about it. If you have some time to make a decision, write down the pros and cons. My guess is, on just about every list, there will be more pros than cons. especially if the opportunity contributes to improving a good relationship, offering you a great physical experience or giving you a positive emotional rush.

When you have a chance to do something big in your life take that chance very seriously. If you're happy and positive and you know the experience will make you happy and positive, the only question you need to answer is this: "Why wouldn't ya?"

POSITIVE THOUGHTS

I will keep my thoughts positive,
because my thoughts become my words.
I will keep my words positive,
because my words become my actions.
I will keep my actions positive,
because my actions become my values.
I will keep my values positive,
because my values become my destiny.

- Unknown

YOUR LIFE BUS

"Attitude is the engine, action is the accelerator in my life bus."

- Glen Daman.

Travis sat in the courtroom wondering how this possibly could have happened. A year ago, he was a successful lawyer with a great family and all the money a 30-year-old could want.

Now, he was sitting in front of a judge waiting for a jail sentence. His career was over, his wife had taken his kids, his world was in shambles.

How could this have possibly happened? And so quickly. After all, this was a guy who had great friends, a country club membership, a nice new Mercedes and invitations to the best parties in town. Just 12 lousy months ago, life was sweet.

But then he met Gordo. Gordo changed his life.

It was pretty tame at first. Gordo was a great guy. His parents had a load of dough so Gordo didn't have to do much. He had an office in a downtown tower that was named after his grandfather and he occasionally answered his phone. He was a vice-president of some kind, but work never seemed to get in the way of a good time. Gordo always had a couple of hours for lunch, always showed up at the best parties and always had a great time. No matter how blessed Travis thought he was, Gordo's life just seemed so much better.

So when Gordo asked Travis to "meet a couple of girls," Travis figured, what could it hurt? And when he and Gordo partied that night, Travis figured the world was at his feet. The girls were gorgeous, and quite young, a lot younger than his 30-something wife, and the small amount of cocain they all snorted together – courtesy of the very wealthy Gordo – just added another level of excitement to the evening.

As Travis sat in the courtroom, waiting to hear the judge's decision, he wanted to blame the drugs. "I mean, come on," he thought. "Gordo could handle them. Why couldn't I? If I could only handle the drugs. If I could have handled it, I wouldn't have left my family to live in that hotel near the dealers. I wouldn't have crashed into that lady's car when I was high. I wouldn't have robbed the convenience store looking for drug money. If I could only handle the drugs."

Sadly, Travis didn't understand his real problem. His problem wasn't the drugs. His problem was the people he brought into his life. He'd never have been near cocaine or any of the other dreadful things he put into his body, if he'd kept an eye on the seats in his life bus.

Gordo was the first to step aboard, but there was also Kelly and Dominique and Shooter and Joey and Ashley. While they climbed aboard, he sent the good people, the people who loved and cared about him, people who had been helping him steer his bus toward success, straight to the back. Eventually, he just tossed some of them off, in order to give more seats to his drinking buddies and his drug dealers and the girls who spent all of his money.

It wasn't the drugs that brought Travis to this courtroom, it was the people he believed were better for his health and happiness than his family and business associates, the friends who had helped him reach a position of authority in the law firm where he worked. Travis lost control of his bus and when he'd cleared out all the good people, he had nothing left but a group of party animals who were hell bent on driving his bus into the ditch.

Are you confused? You thought Travis was a lawyer, not a bus driver? What does a bus have to do with theft and reckless driving and drug abuse?

The answer is: Everything.

We all drive a life bus. After all, it's OUR life. That's it. It's one giant metaphorical bus that we drive from the moment we're born until the day we die. When we start out, we are not in complete control of our bus. It's empty, with the probable exception of our parents and their bags.

As we get older, we add more people to the seats and we eventually take over the wheel, driving it all by ourselves, and taking it even further from our childhood homes. Most of us maintain control, but there are many, like Travis, who find a way to drive their bus right off the asphalt. If you let the wrong people on the bus, or if you simply let the wrong people sit close to you on the bus, you could be asking for trouble.

Now here's how it works: Your life is represented by a bus. You are the driver. You are in total control of where your bus goes. You control it when it stops. You control the speed. You control the fuel you put into it. You control how it is serviced and what road it travels. You even control the direction in which it travels. Most importantly you decide who your passengers are and where they will sit on YOUR bus.

Naturally, the most influential people sit near the front. The people you love more than any of the others, the ones you hold in high regard and the ones you look to for advice and support are the ones who sit the closest to you – the driver. Keep in mind: You never let anyone else drive your bus.

Imagine that the front seats are the ones you can speak to freely and easily and the people in those seats are the ones you see in the mirror above your head. There is also one seat right beside you and this seat is reserved for the person with whom you choose to spend your life.

Now if you're reading this and you are, say, 18 and unmarried, this seat can be occupied, for now, by a parent or mentor. This seat like all seats, can have people move in and out of it. The seat next to me on my life bus is occupied by my wife, Donna and my boys are in the first seat behind me. These are the people dearest to me, who help me navigate the road of my life. My parents are also in the front seats.

My mom, as always, reminds me of right and wrong and what speed to travel (normally she's telling me to slow down) and my dad, is always saying things such as, "Don't turn right down this road son, turn left." I will ask why and often his response is, "Because I've been down this road and it's full of potholes and construction. Oh yeah, and like many of the roads I've traveled, it's also a dead end."

Don't forget, like any bus, it will be very difficult to turn your bus around. In fact, once you head down a certain road, you might never be able to turn your bus at all. This is a classic example of the fact we all have choices. Do we listen to the advice of someone we choose to have sit on our bus or do we turn right anyway? You see, no matter if my dad's advice is right or wrong, it's my choice and no matter the outcome, it's my responsibility; I'm driving. For the record, more often than not the people close to me are right.

Our life bus has many rows of seats and people will come and go, but make no mistake it is up to you who gets on, where they sit and how long they stay. Perhaps the biggest factor between you having a happy, successful life and having a sad, depressing life, is the people you allow on your bus. I believe there are two types of people on our buses and they stay with us throughout our journey through life: good and bad. And again, it's about choices. We have to decide which bus riders are good and which riders are bad. Do they add to our lives or do they subtract?

Remember three things: (1) Choose your friends wisely. (2) Watch out for their baggage because it comes with them and even if they get off the bus, their baggage may be left behind and they'll leave you to deal with it. And (3) always, always, always drive your own bus.

The last one might sound crazy, but there are people out there who allow others to drive their bus for them. That's a guaranteed disaster. As I like to say to one female friend who tends to let her husband drive the bus: "He's driving your bus. You don't let him drive your bus. It's OK to have him on the bus. It's OK to have him sit right up front. But you never let him take the steering wheel."

And watch out for negative people. Too many negative people on your bus is a likely sign that your life is miserable.

And I'll be the first to admit that. I've had many people in my life who were negative people. I've had people work for me who were so negative, I had to let them go. I let them ride on my bus for as long as I could stand it and then just stopped the bus and told them to get off.

Because I have so many people around me who depend on me to make the right decisions, there are times when some people simply have to get off at the next bus stop. Those are people who just cause too much trouble. Negative people, angry people, dishonest people, violent people. There was no room for them on my bus and there shouldn't be any room for them on yours.

Ultimately, I won't have negativity in my life. Because I live life to the 10th Degree, I'll do anything I can to help a person change who honestly wants to change. I'll make suggestions, I'll invite them to a training session. I'll suggest books, I'll talk, I'll do whatever I can. But sometimes there is just no cure for negativity and that's the point where I say, "Enough, off my bus."

Remember, we are the only species on the planet that has the ability to change the way another member of our species thinks, feels or acts. But if, after a period of time, that person has no desire to change, the final decision is yours.

The most important people in your life need to be at the front of your bus. Less important people sit in the middle. Acquaintances and people you only see on occasion can sit at the back. Everybody's baggage has to go underneath with the exception of those people whose luggage is necessary to your existence. That luggage can go overhead, within reach. That baggage includes the love of your family, the trust in your boss, the positive, exciting, intriguing personalities of your closest friends, the beauty of your life.

If your bus is large and full and everyone is together singing Kumbaya, you probably have a great family, wonderful friends and a beautiful life. However, like our friend Travis, your bus can also get jammed up with negative people, people who use you and don't really care about you, people screaming a cacophony into your ear. The driving is impossible. You can't concentrate. You can't keep your bus on the road.

When that happens, it's time to park your bus, determine which riders are causing your bus's engine to hack and cough and get them the heck off the bus.

Our pal Travis didn't get the troublemakers off his bus and eventually they forced his bus off the road. Now, Travis is in a courtroom and his life, his future was in someone else's hands.

You don't want to be Travis. You don't want to lose control. Every single day, take very good care of your bus. Your life is at stake.

Remember, as we take our first steps toward a 10th Degree life, you are the bus driver. You control who is on your life bus. You control the baggage in the luggage carrier. It's your bus and you will be driving it for the rest of your life. Live every day with a positive attitude, make the right choices and keep your bus on the straight and narrow.

As well, remember this: If your life bus seems to be out of control or broken down, it's never too late to take it in for repairs or even for a complete overhaul. There are many service stations and mechanics that specialize in life buses. Call them up and visit them. There are many people on our buses who depend on us. For example, on my bus, my two sons depend on me to drive my bus in the right direction. They depend on it running smoothly. So, if I feel I need the help of a mechanic or the advice from other riders on the bus, I will make sure I go out and get it. Don't ever let pride or ego get in your way. People who love you, depend on that.

THE GOLFER AND THE CADDY

"Your life is not unlike the relationship between a golfer and his caddy. You're the guy, but you will get plenty of advice on how to live or what to do. That's why, when your caddy says hit an eight iron and you reach in the bag, pull out a nine iron and decide to hit it, you have to live with the nine iron. It's because ultimately your name will be on the scorecard. You are the guy. Only you can drive the bus."

- Glen Daman

Book One

PHYSICAL MASTERY

The first step on the road to a 10th Degree life is indeed, a first step. It's time to get in shape. It's time to start walking, running and sweating. It's time to get our bodies ready to do everything we need to do every day.

YOU TUNE YOUR CAR, WHY WOULDN'T YOU TUNE YOUR BODY?

"We spend many hours and thousands of dollars a year to keep our cars tuned and ready to drive. Why wouldn't we make the same commitment of both time and money to tune our own bodies?"

- Glen Daman

THIS IS WHERE IT STARTS
START EARLY, GIVE IT YOUR BEST EVERY DAY

In order to take control of your own world, you must feel good about yourself first. One of the ways to feel good about yourself is to feel good about looking at yourself in the mirror. The best way to do that is eat right and get plenty of exercise.

As well, the best way to feel good from the moment you get out of bed in the morning until the moment you go to bed at night is to be in the best physical condition you can be.

You can't get there by sitting around playing with your Facebook page. Just like the road to the 10th Degree, the road to what I like to call, Physical Mastery, comes from hard work and a commitment to starting your day with exercise and a great breakfast. I have never and will never claim or even insinuate that getting to and then living a 10th Degree Life is easy. As a matter of fact I'll always tell you the opposite. I can still hear my grandfather say: "Hard work has never killed anyone." Reaching the 10th Degree is hard work, but I can guarantee that hard work is very rewarding.

Of all the areas we must master in order to reach The 10th Degree, Physical Mastery is one of the most difficult. Believe me, I know how hard it is to get up every morning and start with a good sweat.

Sure, eating right and exercising sounds simple. I'm sure you've heard it a million times, but it's absolutely true. In fact, it's true for many reasons, including the fact that if you change your lifestyle, get in shape and lose the extra weight or put on the muscle you believe you're lacking, you'll look great in your clothes. Look good, feel good, be healthy. Take control of your physical being. Get the heart rate up and the blood flowing daily, carrying that oxygen that's energizing us! That's Physical Mastery.

How many times have we heard the adage: Your body is your temple? Thousands, I'm sure. Well, that statement is absolutely true. Still, it amazes me how little time we spend on ourselves. Many of us, just don't pay any attention to our own temples.

During my seminars, I tell my audience this: "We spend many hours and thousands of dollars a year to keep our cars tuned and ready to drive. Why wouldn't we make the same commitment of both time and money to tune our own bodies?"

When I think of myself, I think of it this way: If I want to take care of my wife Donna and my sons Brandon and Justin, I first have to take care of Glen. Because if I don't take care of Glen, then a time will come – a time much sooner than I would like - when I won't be there to take care of Brandon, Justin and Donna.

It's selfishness of the first order, but as Dipak Gupta, a professor of public administration and urban studies at San Diego State University and author of Path to Collective Madness: A Study in Social Order and Political Pathology, wrote: This is, "Selfish selflessness." and it always reminds me that you have to take care of yourself first, before you are capable of taking care of anybody else.

MY DAILY ROUTINE

I can't expect you to begin the often difficult task of attaining Physical Mastery without telling you how I spend my day. It's only fair that I work just as hard as you do in order to reach a mutual goal. My question for you, once again, is: "If I could change your life for the better in 60 minutes a day, would you give me that 60 minutes?"

It all starts with your alarm. Mine goes off at 5:00 a.m. I'm not going to demand that you join what the brilliant Robin Sharma, author of The Greatness Guide, calls, "The 5 O'clock Club," I'm just asking for 60 minutes at the beginning of your entire day.

For example, if you normally rise at 8 a.m., then I want you to get up and at 'em at 7:00 a.m. I believe in the morning workout because it jump-starts the metabolism early in the day. And there are no excuses. Get it done. I don't know about you, but if I allow myself to make excuses, I can come up with all sorts of excuses, throughout the day, not to do my workouts. Frankly, there is nothing quite like the feeling you get when you jump out of the shower at 6 a.m., wide awake with your workout finished and you still have the full day ahead of you. Now, let's be honest here. If, for some reason, you can't do a morning workout, don't put the book down and quit. Just make sure you get it in sometime before the end of the day.

Now I'm usually awake before my alarm because after years and years of early mornings, I'm used to it. I suspect that for many of you, this is going to take some getting used to. So start off easy. Get up 30 minutes early and work your way up to 60 minutes.

When I hop out of bed, the first thing I do is I put on my gear and either go for a run or a very brisk walk. I do something to get my heart rate up. If I'm in a hotel room, I might forego the run and do jumping jacks on the spot or push and sit ups, with SportsCentre on TV, but every morning, the first thing I do is get physical in order to get my heart rate up.

You get that heart rate up and you get the blood moving and work up a nice little sweat. When you get the blood moving, you start carrying oxygen to every part of your body. That early-morning oxygen gives me energy for the rest of the day.

I always tell people that I do 30-45 minutes, minimum, every single day (once again, starting out your minimum should be 20 minutes). But, of course, I never penalize myself for doing a little extra. If I feel I have time and I'm particularly enjoying my workout I'll go 15 minutes to 30 minutes longer. You can never work too hard or sweat too much.

However, I feel your pain. If you are new to this, it would be unrealistic for me to expect someone who has never spent any time working out, let alone working out at 5 in the morning, to do this 30-45 minutes a day, every day. So here's what I'd suggest: Give me 10 minutes a day. Just go for a walk. Make it five minutes out and five minutes back. Work up to 10 minutes out and 10 minutes back. It won't be long before you're 15 minutes out and 15 minutes back

So if you're doing nothing now, see your doctor, make sure your fit enough for physical activity and get to work. It's important that you get going, get rockin' and rollin'.

Now, I know what some of you are thinking. Five o'clock in the morning? Every day. Run? Come on, Glen, that's crazy.

Every time I speak to a group, I get this question: "You know what Glen, I'm just not motivated enough on my own."

My immediate response is a simple one: "Great, get a trainer."

More often than not, my inquisitor will reply: "I can't." And I just say, "Why not? Don't ever tell me you can't. We can. We always can. We may choose not to, but we always have choices and in this case, the choice is simple: Hire a trainer."

Then I almost always get this response: "Because a trainer costs $40 an hour and I can't afford that. If I try to work out with a trainer for an hour a week, four times a week, that's $120 a week, $480 a month. I can't afford that."

That's when I ask them about their car. I say to them, "You can go ahead and Google this, but the average person spends somewhere between $300 and $400 per month on maintenance to their automobile. Why do you do that?" The response is always the same: "Well, Glen, it's important, I need it to get to and from work, it's my livelihood, I drive my kids around, it's important that I have a well-tuned car."

"That's true," I tell them, "But if you drop dead tomorrow because you're unhealthy, because your own engine has broken down, is that a good thing or a bad thing? Personally, I think it's a bad thing. You'll spend $400 on maintenance on your car every month, but you won't spend that on your own health. We spend more time and attention on our flower gardens, our vehicles and our pets, than we do on ourselves. That's borderline insanity, don't you think. You place more value on an automobile than you do on your own body. How did we ever reach a point where that was, somehow, logical thinking?

Don't ever tell me you can't. You can. You may choose not to, but you can. And don't even tell me that you'll try. Because "try" rhymes with "cry." I don't believe in it. Don't give me a lackadaisical effort, just do it. I guarantee, it will be the best decision you ever make in your life.

GRANDPA

My grandfather or "grandpa" as I called him was my idol, mentor and, at times, my best friend.

I'll admit, I was not always easy to deal with as a young guy and my mom often relied on my grandpa to be that father figure, the dad I didn't have when my real father was gone. Well, he accepted that role with gusto and to this day is the single biggest reason that I was able to cope with the fact my father had left us. Like most kids, I didn't always appreciate it then but I sure do now.

Both grandparents filled in while my mom was working, and they were especially important to us when we were on summer vacation from school. I still can't believe how grandpa could come up with projects around the yard whenever I wanted to sleep in. He could find more work on my days off than anyone ever in the history of mankind.

But he did this: He taught me the value of the term "work ethic." He would often say, "hard work never killed anyone." Of course, I was sure I'd be the first, but then again I'm also sure I'm not the only kid who was ever put in that position on a farm. Cutting grass, cleaning barns, painting sheds you name it, there was always something to do.

When I got older, I found out that grandpa was very gifted. He had this kind of fifth sense that I'd always been told only your mom had. Grandpa was extremely good at knowing when I was out late with my friends. When I was in my late teens and out for a night on the town with my best buddies, David, Mark and Brett, I'd come home in the wee hours of the morning and he would make the walk over to the trailer well before 7 a.m. and wake me up. I can here him now: "You up son?" I would reply, "Grandpa its Saturday I have nothing to get up for and I just got home, I'm sleeping."

That's when grandpa would utter a famous grandpa line, a remark that I've never forgotten: "If you want to fish all night you have to dry your nets in the morning." Now, I don't know how a farmer from Manitoba knew anything about drying fishing nets, but out of respect I never asked.

This saying has been passed down from my grandpa to me to my son Justin. Justin and I talk about Physical Mastery every day. It's importance in your journey to the 10th Degree carries the same magnitude as Mental Mastery, Professional Mastery or Relationship Mastery.

And if you ever wanted to know where my 5 a.m. rule comes from: It's grandpa. Remember, "If you want to fish all night you have to dry your nets in the morning."

OVER THE EDGE

I wasn't always committed to a fitness program. I'll be the first to admit that. But a horrible experience involving a very dear friend, forced me to re-evaluate my entire lifestyle. It was this experience that put me over the edge.

My very close friend, Ken, died suddenly from a heart attack. He was 36.

He left his widow to look after his three girls, with help from his parents and his in-laws. I came to the abrupt realization that I was out of shape and needed to take a serious look at my lifestyle.

By appearance, Ken looked fit, but I knew that I sure wasn't. I'm 5'9" and at the time, I weighed 195 pounds. It was time for a change. So the first thing I did was quit smoking. It was my first step toward real mastery. I learned at that time that if something doesn't add to our health, it will take away from our health.

It's no different than putting fuel into our cars. We will happily put high octane fuels into our automobiles in order to get better fuel mileage, but when it comes to our own bodies, we'll think nothing of smoking cigarettes, drinking alcoholic beverages in excess and putting junk food into our bodies. I understand addictions, but this isn't about addictions. Your body is your vehicle for life. You have to look after it.

And while it's important to consider the vanity aspect of looking good – I know I look a lot better and my clothes fit a lot better now that I weigh 170 pounds -- it has less to do with vanity and it has almost everything to do with feeling good!

So Physical Mastery is more than just getting up early to work out. We also have to consider what we're putting into our bodies.

We must eat foods that are rich in vitamins and minerals and we must eat our first meal of the day early in the morning. Physical Mastery as stated earlier, should happen first thing in the morning because it kick-starts your metabolism.

I'm not a doctor. I don't even play one on TV. But in discussions with doctors and nutritionists, I've learned that when you work out and then eat a good breakfast, first thing in the morning, you're kick-starting your metabolism for the day. Your engine is now running. And it will run all day at a high level as long as you feed it with good foods, with plenty of fruits and vegetables and all your basics.

Here's a tip: Follow the Canadian Food Guide! Or the US Food Guide. It's very simple. It will give a daily regimen for eating right and for putting the correct fuels into your body. And if you start that engine early in the morning, you will feel better for the entire day.

THE CANADIAN FOOD GUIDE

By having the amount and type of food recommended and by following the tips in *Canada's Food Guide* will help:

- Meet your needs for vitamins, minerals and other nutrients.
- Reduce your risk of obesity, type 2 diabetes, heart disease, certain types of cancer and osteoporosis.
- Contribute to your overall health and vitality.

What is one Food Guide Serving?
Look at the examples below.

Vegetables and Fruit
Fresh, frozen or canned vegetables - 125 mL (½ cup)
Leafy vegetables - 250 mL (1 cup)
Fresh, frozen or canned fruits - 1 fruit or 125 mL (½ cup)
100% Juice - 125 mL (½ cup)

Grain Products
Bread - 1 slice (35 g)
Bagel - ½ bagel (45 g)
Flat breads - ½ pita or ½ tortilla (35 g)
Cooked rice, bulgur or quinoa - 125 mL (½ cup)
Cereal Cold: 30 g Hot: 175 mL (¾ cup)
Cooked pasta or couscous 125 mL (½ cup)

Milk and Alternatives
Milk or powered milk (reconstituted) - 250 mL (1 cup)
Canned milk (evaporated) - 125 mL (½ cup)

Fortified soy beverage - 250 mL (1 cup)

Yogurt - 175 g (¾ cup)

Cheese - 50 g (1 ½ oz.)

Meat and Alternatives

Cooked fish, shellfish, poultry, lean meat - 75 g (2 ½ oz.)/125 mL (½ cup)

Cooked legumes - 175 mL (3/4 cup)

Tofu - 150 g or 175 mL (¾ cup)

Eggs - 2 eggs

Peanut or nut butters - 30 mL (2 Tbsp)

Shelled nuts and seeds - 60 mL (¼ cup)

Oils and Fats

Include a small amount – 30 to 45 mL (2 to 3 Tbsp) – of unsaturated fat each day. This includes oil used for cooking, salad dressings, margarine and mayonnaise.

Use vegetable oils such as canola, olive and soybean.

Choose soft margarines that are low in saturated and trans fats.

Limit butter, hard margarine, lard and shortening.

Make each Food Guide Serving count.

Wherever you are - at home, at school, at work or when eating out!

Eat at least one dark green and one orange vegetable each day.

Go for dark green vegetables such as broccoli, romaine lettuce and spinach.

Go for orange vegetables such as carrots, sweet potatoes and winter squash.

Choose vegetables and fruit prepared with little or no added fat, sugar or salt.

Enjoy vegetables steamed, baked or stir-fried instead of deep-fried.

Have vegetables and fruit more often than juice.

Make at least half of your grain products whole grain each day.

Eat a variety of whole grains such as barley, brown rice, oats, quinoa and wild rice.

Enjoy whole grain breads, oatmeal or whole wheat pasta.

Choose grain products that are lower in fat, sugar or salt.

Compare the Nutrition Facts table on labels to make wise choices.

Enjoy the true taste of grain products. When adding sauces or spreads, use small amounts.

Drink skim, 1%, or 2% milk each day.

Have 500 mL (2 cups) of milk every day for adequate vitamin D.

Drink fortified soy beverages if you do not drink milk.

Select lower fat milk alternatives.

Compare the Nutrition Facts table on yogurts or cheeses to make wise choices.

Have meat alternatives such as beans, lentils and tofu often.

Eat at least two Food Guide Servings of fish each week. *

Choose fish such as char, herring, mackerel, salmon, sardines and trout.

Select lean meat and alternatives prepared with little or no added fat or salt.

Trim the visible fat from meats. Remove the skin on poultry.

Use cooking methods such as roasting, baking or poaching that require little or no added fat.

If you eat luncheon meats, sausages or packaged meats, choose those lower in salt (sodium) and fat.

- Health Canada provides advice for limiting exposure to mercury from certain types of fish. Refer to www.healthcanada.gc.ca for the latest information.

Enjoy a variety of foods from the four food groups.

Satisfy your thirst with water!

Drink water regularly. It's a calorie-free way to quench your thirst.

Drink more water in hot weather or when you are very active.

Advice for different ages and stages.

Children

Following *Canada's Food Guide* helps children grow and thrive.

Young children have small appetites and need calories for growth and development.

Serve small nutritious meals and snacks each day.

Do not restrict nutritious foods because of their fat content. Offer a variety of foods from the four food groups.

Most of all...be a good role model.

Women of childbearing age

All women who could become pregnant and those who are pregnant or breastfeeding need a multivitamin containing **folic**

acid every day.

Pregnant women need to ensure that their multivitamin also contains **iron**. A health care professional can help you find the multivitamin that's right for you.

Pregnant and breastfeeding women need more calories. Include an extra 2 to 3 Food Guide Servings each day.

Here are two examples:

Have fruit and yogurt for a snack, or

Have an extra slice of toast at breakfast and an extra glass of milk at supper.

Men and women over 50

The need for **vitamin D** increases after the age of 50.

In addition to following *Canada's Food Guide*, everyone over the age of 50 should take a daily vitamin D supplement of 10 µg (400 IU).

How do I count Food Guide Servings in a meal?

Here is an example:

Vegetable and beef stir-fry with rice, a glass of milk and an apple for dessert

250 mL (1 cup) mixed broccoli, carrot and sweet red pepper = 2 **Vegetables and Fruit** Food Guide Servings

75 g (2 ½ oz.) lean beef = 1 **Meat and Alternatives** Food Guide Serving

250 mL (1 cup) brown rice = 2 **Grain Products** Food Guide Servings

5 mL (1 tsp) canola oil = part of your **Oils and Fats** intake

for the day

250 mL (1 cup) 1% milk = 1 **Milk and Alternatives** Food Guide Serving

1 apple = 1 **Vegetables and Fruit** Food Guide Serving

Eat well and be active today and every day!
The benefits of eating well and being active include:

Better overall health.

Lower risk of disease.

A healthy body weight.

Feeling and looking better.

More energy.

Stronger muscles and bones.

Be active

To be active every day is a step towards better health and a healthy body weight.

Canada's Physical Activity Guide recommends building 30 to 60 minutes of moderate physical activity into daily life for adults and at least 90 minutes a day for children and youth. You don't have to do it all at once. Add it up in periods of at least 10 minutes at a time for adults and five minutes at a time for children and youth.

Start slowly and build up.

Eat well

Another important step towards better health and a healthy

body weight is to follow *Canada's Food Guide* by:

Eating the recommended amount and type of food each day.

Limiting foods and beverages high in calories, fat, sugar or salt (sodium) such as cakes and pastries, chocolate and candies, cookies and granola bars, doughnuts and muffins, ice cream and frozen desserts, french fries, potato chips, nachos and other salty snacks, alcohol, fruit flavoured drinks, soft drinks, sports and energy drinks, and sweetened hot or cold drinks.

Read the label

Compare the Nutrition Facts table on food labels to choose products that contain less fat, saturated fat, trans fat, sugar and sodium.

Keep in mind that the calories and nutrients listed are for the amount of food found at the top of the Nutrition Facts table.

Limit trans fat

When a Nutrition Facts table is not available, ask for nutrition information to choose foods lower in trans and saturated fats.

Take a step today...

Have breakfast every day. It may help control your hunger later in the day.

Walk wherever you can – get off the bus early, use the stairs.

Benefit from eating vegetables and fruit at all meals and as snacks.

Spend less time being inactive such as watching TV or playing computer games.

Request nutrition information about menu items when eating out to help you make healthier choices.

Enjoy eating with family and friends!

Take time to eat and savour every bite!

For more information, interactive tools or additional copies visit Canada 's Food Guide on-line at: http://www.healthcanada. gc.ca/foodguide

REACHING PHYSICAL MASTERY

When you've started your workout routine and learned to eat right, you're well on your way to Physical Mastery.

As an example, another aspect of having Physical Mastery is your ability to sleep. Sleep, is extremely important, but I assure you, if you get up at 5 a.m., then you spend somewhere between 20 minutes and an hour every morning working out, then you follow it up by eating a proper breakfast, you know your engine is burning and it will burn all day. Eat well during the day, have a great attitude and work hard and I promise, if you make that your lifestyle, then in the early evening -- for me it's about 10:30 -- you'll sleep like a baby. You're living a healthy life and you will sleep like a rock. By 5 a.m. the next morning you'll be revitalized, rejuvenated and ready to go out and do it again.

Keep it up, and your life will change. You will be successful. You will be healthy. There is absolutely no doubt.

In the meantime, I'm not crazy. I might talk like a crazy person sometimes, but I know the difference between reality and my own personal commitment to health and happiness. Listen, I know we're all human. We all have that thing called the "H" factor. Do I have the odd slice of cheesecake? Yes. Do I have the odd bottle of beer? Of course I do. I enjoy the world's best beers often! Is that in the Canadian Food Guide, the U.S. Food Guide, or the Swedish Food Guide? Not that I know of, but if you're otherwise healthy and doing it right most of the time it's OK to enjoy yourself once in a while.

I mean that. You can still enjoy life. I still have a bag of chips every now and again. Mind you, I don't eat the whole bag. I have a couple of cups and I don't do it every day. But every once in a while, indulging oneself in the odd potato chip or piece of cheesecake is not going to mean you're doomed.

One of the things I love to do in my life is just sit down and enjoy a milkshake with my kids. There's nothing wrong with that. But I used to have milkshakes every day. As my mother still tells me, "We must do things in moderation." A milkshake-a-day is not a good way to reach physical mastery.

In essence, this is a lot like our Life Line: Never get too high, never got too low, get in a groove and keep to it. Physical Mastery is just so, so important.

MARTIAL ARTS

This is the reason I named this program the 10th Degree.

I've been around the martial arts scene since I was a teenager and I've spent a great deal of time with Master Malcolm Edwards. Master Edwards has been a part of my life since 1988 and he's trained my son, Justin, to not only be the reigning national champion, but a world championship medal winner for Team Canada.

I've been involved with Baes Martial Arts in Winnipeg for many years and today I'm actually part of the management side of the club. So even though it's been a long period in which I didn't train, I've been around the beauty and physicality of the sport for a great portion of my life. When you listen to a master's teachings, day in and day out, for many years, it sinks in and there is very little doubt that it played a major role in my ability to reach Physical Mastery. Master Malcolm Edwards is a dear friend of mine who I speak with on an almost daily basis. He is a big reason for my continued journey at the 10th Degree.

Master Edwards teaches his people that if you want to get something from your body, then your mind and your physical being have to match up. That's why we talk about mental mastery as well as Physical Mastery because they have to go together. Mastery is clearly a martial arts term and is the reason I refer to the five points leading to the 10th Degree as "Mastery." I would suggest to anyone to get involved in martial arts. Not only is it a great way to keep in shape physically, but mentally as well.

"When we focus on our goals it gives us purpose. We can't however forget to enjoy the ride. The ride is what our memories are made of. So have a purpose and enjoy every step!"

- Glen Daman

THOUGHTS ON WORKING OUT

When I'm working out especially hard, I like to alternate my routine. I try to run three days a week minimum.

However, if someone wants to run more than three days a week and their doctor is OK with that then that's just fantastic.

There is an 84-year-old woman in California who runs five miles a day. She's 84! Fantastic! Personally, if you're asking me, I run three days a week for three or more miles every time and I stretch before and after. The days I don't run, I lift light weights with plenty of repetitions.

I'm not interested in bulking up, but some people are and that's great, too. For me, I do light weights just for toning and for keeping my muscles trained. That's it. Five days a week.

"Here are three things that will get us through stressful times, every time: Laugh often, talk to friends and exercise."

- Glen Daman

PLAYING TEAM SPORTS

It sure doesn't hurt to have a favourite sport, a sport you love to play. For me, it was ice hockey. I played at every level growing up, house league, community club, traveling teams. I enjoyed it, every moment of it. It's probably the most fun I've had in my life. There is no pressure on me when I play, but again it's all about the relationships you have.

I met so many great people through hockey and, to this day, I'm still in contact with many of them. I learned the importance of "team play" from playing hockey. I was often a team captain or an assistant captain but that just taught me leadership and the importance of having a number of people counting on you all the time.

Team sport teaches us that it's not all about ourselves. It not only helps you understand physical mastery at an early age, but it really helps with our Relationship Mastery, because there is a lot of give and take. It's not about you, it's about you doing things for others to help the team win.

When the puck goes in the net it's not the defenseman's fault. The defenseman was simply part of a series of mistakes all over the ice that resulted in a goal being scored against your team.

In football, if a defensive back is beaten for a touchdown, it wasn't just the defensive back who allowed the other team to score, but the defensive line, the rush, the linebackers, all the coverages. In team sports, it's not the individual. It's everybody working together, doing things correctly and working hard to help the entire team earn a victory. Team sports are phenomenal, not just for kids, but for everybody. I believe if we got our kids involved in team sports or sports of any kind we would have less crime involving our youth of today. It gives young people a purpose and goals and gives them something to go to multiple times a week keeping them occupied both physically and mentally.

"Playing a team sport teaches us that everyone on the team needs to beat with one heart and without all of us being a part of it, we'll never be strong."

- Glen Daman

YOU'RE NOW HEALTHY

Physical Mastery is all about being healthy. It's not measured with a scale, a wart on your face, or the size of your nose. If you need proof of that, just look at my nose. I've broken it three times. My mom wants everyone to know that I wasn't born like this. But it's not about who you see in the mirror, it's about who you see in the mirror on the inside.

Now make no mistake, I want you to be healthy. I want you to go to your doctor and have your doctor say, "Wow! You're healthy, your blood pressure is good and your heart is strong." But you also have to be happy about you.

That is Physical Mastery. I believe that by getting up at 5 a.m. every single day, being done my workout, out of my shower and ready to start my mental mastery before I leave for work, I've done what needs to be done to be a master of my physical being. If I'm done all of that by 7 a.m., I'm ready to rock and roll and most of the people I have to deal with during the day aren't even out of bed yet. When I get that done, I know I have an unfair advantage.

"To be a master of your physical being, you have to look at your life like a prizefighter looks at his next fight. You're getting yourself physically ready every day just like a prizefighter prepares for his next opponent except we fight every day. If a prizefighter isn't physically ready for his opponent, he could get killed. If you aren't ready for every day life, it could kill you."

- Glen Daman

IT WILL CHANGE YOUR LIFE

Physical Mastery, if attained, will change your life, imagine you will eat healthier, sleep better and get the heart rate up 5 days a week minimum. Your blood will be flowing early bringing oxygen and giving you more energy than ever before. You will feel better about yourself and it will improve your attitude. Physical Mastery is a important ingredient in attaining all the masteries required for a 10th Degree life.

I've received many e-mails and letters and I'm always being approached by all sorts of people from all walks of life who have practiced Physical Mastery, and they all tell me their stories, stories that simply confirm the importance of physical mastery to living a 10th Degree life.

Book Two

MENTAL MASTERY

We're feeling good about ourselves and we enjoy getting up early in the morning, having our 20-30-minute workout and then enjoying a solid, healthy breakfast. Now it's time to get our minds functioning for the day ahead.

BE CAREFUL WITH WORDS

"We are the only being on the planet that has the ability to change the way another member of the species thinks, feels and/or acts simply by the words with which we speak. So choose your words carefully."

- Glen Daman

WE LOOK GOOD AND FEEL GOOD. NOW IT'S TIME TO EXERCISE AND TAME OUR GREY CELLS

MENTAL MASTERY

Ever noticed that when you're happy, things that take place around you seem to move in slow motion, to float on air, to always come up in your favour?

Funny thing about happiness and its trappings. When you're happy, people around you are happy. When you're happy, you bring out the best in people. But when you're in the dumps, frowning, complaining about your job, bitter about things that no one else really understands, people around you get tired, angry and less than productive.

Happiness is contagious as Rhonda Byrnes writes in the section on Laws of Attraction in her book, *The Secret*. Still, we're not always happy. We're not always outgoing. We don't always attack our day with a positive attitude.

Now, let's be clear. If you've changed your life by mastering the physicality of your life, every day will be better. That goes without saying. If you get off to a great start, by working out and eating a nutritious breakfast, you've taken the first steps toward a happy, friendly, outgoing, positive day.

After all, it's quite difficult to feel badly about what's in front of you when you've had your workout and eaten a good, nutritious breakfast. For one thing, you're going to feel better about yourself, but let's not be naïve here, we can get stuck in a rut and physical mastery isn't always enough.

Things happen to us, often on a daily basis, that can bring us down and take away our motivation. How we respond to and then what we do with all the things that happen to us during our day, are situations we can prepare for mentally before we get to work or school. Like a boxer prepares mentally for a fight or a football player for a big game, we can prepare mentally for our day. The fact is, and never forget this, we have a choice. We can approach our day and the people with whom we deal, from a positive, trusting, happy and empathetic point of view or we can be angry, unhappy, bitter and selfish. Like everything else in our lives, we all have that choice.

Mental Mastery is about making the right choice.

In fact, Mental Mastery is simply this: "We get up everyday. How are we going to attack our day?"

First and foremost, I believe that reading is leading and leading is reading. Read something every single day that gives you inspiration, that lifts you up, that will give you a head-start to your day and give you the attitude that's required to be the absolute best you can be. Fill your head full of motivating, inspirational and positive thoughts.

Think about it: You have just finished getting that blood flowing with a great morning exercise routine and you've followed it up with a healthy breakfast. Now, you add in positive, uplifting and motivational reading. What a recipe. Where is your attitude now?

Good or bad? That's right, it's GREAT!

It sounds very simple, and it is. Let me remind you the steps that help you reach the 10th Degree are simple or else I wouldn't be doing them.

Whatever it is you do for a living, I don't care if you cut grass at a golf course, if you're a painter, whatever it is you do for your personal profession, I believe you want to be the best that you can be at that. And that's the deal. Mental Mastery is about being the best you can be.

POISONED BY NEGATIVITY

Our world is so, so, so poisoned by negativity, whether it's at the water cooler, on the TV and radio news, in the newspaper you pick up, it doesn't matter: The media knows and has known for a long, long time that negativity sells.

I can pick up the newspaper any day of the week and I will guarantee you that the majority of that newspaper is about a war that's going on, or an accident that took place, or a break and enter down the street, or a shooting, or a stabbing. It will tell you that the economy's down, or your currency is down, or your oil stock is down... It's ALL negativity. It will tell you that your neighbor is a crook, that the politicians are incompetent, that the local football coach is a jerk and the players do drugs. The newspapers will write all this, even if it isn't true. Because like gossip in a school yard, that's what sells for all forms of media – newspapers, TV, radio. Negativity sells.

For the mainstream media, bad, even manufactured bad, is good. Take your average meteorologist. He or she will always report that there is a 30 per cent chance of showers never a 70 per cent chance of sunshine. It's like a disease.

Now I'll be the first to admit that everyone needs information, but there are plenty of positive places to go for that information without being bombarded by the negative. If you're a football fan, go to the web and click on www.nfl.com or www.cfl.com. You'll get all the information you need, game reports, stats, even great video, but you won't have to listen to a screed from some sportswriter who has never played a down of football, selling negativity to the masses. Same goes for local issues, hobbies, airline schedules and movie times. The information is all available on the web, without having to wallow in the negativity that destroys lives. Always remember this: The vast majority of all human beings traffic in negativity.

Think about it. When one of your friends has a story (better known as gossip) that they can't wait to tell you, is it usually a positive or a negative story? Want examples? Here are a few (the names have been changed to protect the innocent), "Bob and Kathy are breaking up!" "Tommy got cut from the baseball team!" "Eddie got fired!"

If you've partaken in water cooler gossip at work you'll know that these are better sellers than "Young Tommy hit two home runs," or "Eddie got a raise." However, if you are truly serious about living a 10th Degree life then let me give you a couple of suggestions: 1) Don't give the person who is dealing in gossip an audience and 2) work on cutting negativity out of your life.

Now, I know what you're thinking: Glen that person dealing in negativity is my Mom or Glen that person is my best friend. If that's the case then you need to sit that person down and explain that you have no room in your life for negativity. If the conversation is not positive or doesn't add to your life in some way, then you don't want to hear it. Believe me when I say there are more than enough positive stories and miracles out there – on a daily basis! – that there is no risk of running out of things to talk about. If the person is not close to you then just stay away.

Meanwhile, I know we all think we aren't negative but I can assure you that we are. At least, at one time or another. Work on eliminating negative words from your vocabulary. Granted, that is much easier to say than do and I have to admit, I still work on this every day and I expect I will be working on it until I breathe my last breath. However, if we all worked on cutting this cancerous negativity out of our lives, can you imagine the kind of world we'd be living in? I heard that, and you're right. We'd live in a 10th Degree world and how great would that be?

Now I believe, like my grandmother used to say to me, "It's really simple: Garbage in, garbage out." So we have to weigh and balance and approach all this negativity. At some point, we have to stop poisoning ourselves with this all day long. We have to stop poisoning our children, for that matter. There is a statistic that's staggering of how many hours of violence and murders that our children witness on television. Children who watch a lot of TV, especially TV news, cartoons and drama are witness to a least 8,000 murders before they get out of Grade 6.

According to Dr. George Comstock, professor of communication at Syracuse University, children's cartoons are among the most violent of formats. The best count is 14 violent incidents per hour, compared to about six for general audience programming. According to Comstock, Cartoons make violent behavior particularly attractive to children. They almost always show violence as achieving a sought-for goal, and as the normal way to behave. Children imitate those who succeed, and in cartoons, violence succeeds.

Violence is more prevalent in children's shows. Dr. Barbara Wilson, Vice Provost of the University of Illinois at Urbana-Champaign, conducted a large scale study examining physical violence on television from 1994 to 1997. Of more than 3,000 programs airing on 23 channels, she found that nearly 70 per cent of children's programs contained physical violence while less than 60 per cent of non-children's shows did. There are two observations Dr. Wilson made from these percentages. First, violence is a staple in most fictional programming on television today. But second, physical violence is even more likely to be portrayed in shows targeted to children aged 12 and under. Many of these programs, of course, are cartoons.

According to the American Psychological Association, "an average twelve-year- old has seen 8,000 murders and 100,000 acts of violence on network television." According to Dr. Aletha Huston's 1992 study titled "Big World, Small Screen: The role of Television in American Society," by the time a child is eighteen years old, he or she will witness on television (with average viewing time) 200,000 acts of violence including 40,000 murders.

But as corporate media has made clear to us, negativity sells so I want to ask you a question. How many births do you think occur on average, every day in our world? According to the American Medical Association, 340,500 births occur each day around the world. Isn't that one of the greatest miracles? How many calves were born on a farm today? How many piglets, how many chickens, how many whatever? How many births occurred in the ocean? Miracles, all of them.

How many firemen, around the world, saved a life yesterday? How many policeman saved a life? How many wallets were found on the street yesterday and were returned with all the money in them.

Is that in the paper? Is that on CNN? Not likely.

Now, I'm not saying "Next On Oprah," or that Glen Daman is about to change the world, I'm saying that if people spent 15 minutes a day picking up a positive book by one of the greatest authors of our time – Mandino, Blanchard, Sharma, Chopra, Oprah, there are so many of them – would the world not be a better place?

After all, these are books that not only discuss, but go on to explain the positive: Only the positive. How you can be a better person and how you can attack your day with a smile and a kind word if you're gorging yourself with negativity all day long? Books by Mandino, Sharma and Blanchard will take you in a new direction. The writing is beautiful and every word is uplifting. There is absolutely no negativity.

Simply put, these people changed my life. I find, even today, that my attitude will take a turn for the worse, if I go days without my morning read. Just like a professional athlete, you must practice this routine every day or you will get out of practice and slowly return to ordinary. You will lose the 10th Degree. How often do you think the greats practice their professions? Think of people such as Rice, Montana, Favre, Gretzky and Agassi. Think of how hard and often they work at their games.

Here is a tip to add enjoyment when reading a good book. I encourage you to carry a highlighter and highlight the lines, paragraphs or pages you like the best. Then when you complete the book go back and on a piece of paper write out those highlighted portions. Then place your sheet of paper in the book so you can read your notes on the book anytime you want.

Still, I'll admit that reading may not be enough to bring you to mental mastery so here's another suggestion: Learn a new skill. Why not do yourself a favour and, at the same time, help yourself out?

Why not learn something new? That's right, learn another language, learn to cook, learn to knit, learn to draw. How good would you feel about yourself if you became fluent in a second or third language, something different than your mother tongue? Would that add to your positive attitude or take something away? Yep, that's what I thought.

In the end, you'll benefit and while it might not get you off to the positive start to your day that a piece by Robin Sharma or Og Mandino will, it's still good for you, makes you a better person and gets those grey cells working first thing in the morning.

I was once asked, "What's the most important thing you can ever be given?" and I replied, "A book." My inquisitor looked at me incredulously and asked: "Well what if you were starving on the street?" and I played along. I said, "OK, if I was starving on the street and somebody offered you a sandwich or a great book, I'd take the book. Because even if you took the sandwich, it would cure your hunger for a short time but you would be hungry again. If you read that book, it might stay with you forever and it could change your life, forever."

The best gifts I've ever been given – that's in my entire life – are books. Not jewelry or cars or airline tickets, but books. Other than my children, books are probably the greatest gifts I can receive. If I'd lost my wallet and was hungry, I could quite easily go to a soup kitchen and have a nice bowl of soup, but stand in Chapters and see how long it takes for somebody to buy you a book. That isn't likely to happen. Books are valuable, hopeful and precious, a playground for your mind. A book will stay with you forever. Read something inspirational or positive every single day of your life.

I always loved to sit and colour with my boys, or do a puzzle. That's good for you, too, Every day you must do something that gets your brain working and yet takes you away from the negativity. There is no cure for written negativity other than staying away from it. You should run away from it as fast as you can.

I don't read the newspaper. I used to, but it reached a point where nothing in it was good for me, nothing in it was good for my attitude. Now, I'll admit that I do read the sports section, but it's reached the point where none of that is very uplifting either. Instead of reading about wonderful athletic achievements by amateur athletes and young people, all we get now is professional sport and the trials and tribulations those people face every day: drugs, drunk driving, domestic abuse, newspaper columnists who pass social judgments on athletes and coaches, most of whom they've never met. It has reached a point where the sports section and the entertainment sections are no better for us than the news sections.

Now, for the sake of full disclosure, I am a fan of the Toronto Maple Leafs, a professional hockey team that hasn't won a championship since 1967. So when I read about my favourite team, I seldom read anything positive. I have considered starting a paper of only positive stories in the news and sports sections. What do you think? You're right, it won't sell. I will have to wait until The 10th Degree spreads around the world.

My co-author Scott Taylor, a sports writer of some renown, once suggested to me that all a man – and a woman – needs to get through life is a favourite sports team and a favourite rock band.

My first response was, "Why is that?"

So he explained: "Because you've always got your ball team no matter how bad things are at work, no matter how bad your life is at home, you can always sit down and follow your team. And that may be a hockey team in Canada, or a soccer team in Britain, but wherever it is in the world, you've got YOUR team.

"Then, let's say you've just had enough of the world. It's been a lousy day at work and the people around you just weren't as positive as you were. No matter how good your attitude is at the start of the day, you will occasionally hit a time and/or a place where the people around you just don't share your enthusiasm for life. If that's the case, you can just go home, put your music on and listen to your favourite rock band. I've always believed that if you have a rock band and a ball team you can get through it all."

I told Scott that I loved it. It was a great idea.

Sadly, in this world, most people are subjected, better yet, immersed, in negativity and there are times when we wonder why we say to ourselves: "You know, I don't want to hang out with Bob anymore because Bob's just so negative. All he does is talk negatively about people. He talks about all the bad politicians and crooked cops and lousy parking meters and rotten laws and really, all the things he reads every day in the newspaper. He talks about all the things that just get me down and I'm tired of it."

Not surprisingly, that's how this planet is built, and to me it's very, very sad. But I try to look at my day this way: What can I do to help a guy like Bob have a more positive outlook on life. Instead of just ignoring him, my first thought is to try to find a way to help him out.

It's not impossible and it's always worth the effort, even if it seems that a guy like Bob tends to like his miserable life.

The world is an amazing place. If you start the day with a positive outlook and carry that outlook everywhere you go, somebody is going to notice. Somebody is going to latch on to your happiness and success, and your bright, sunny attitude and just tag along for the ride. Being positive and happy, having the right attitude toward life, will never, ever go unnoticed or unrewarded. Even if those rewards are only warm feelings and added confidence.

One of my favourite quotes in the world, and the author is unknown, is this: "We will not be remembered by our words, but by our kind deeds. They say it takes a minute to find a special person, an hour to appreciate them, a day to love them, but an entire lifetime to forget them. Life is not measured by the breath we take, but by the moments that take our breath away."

There is no room in our lives for negativity. It simply does not need to be there, and like some of the incurable diseases on our planet there is no cure for negativity. Remember this: The only cure for negativity is to stay away from it.

It's tough to do, I understand that, but it you took 15 minutes a day and just got nothing but positive stuff driven into your brain, would that make you better or worse? To answer my own question bluntly, "I know it would make you better."

Wouldn't that be amazing, wouldn't the world be amazing, if we could all be positive all the time? Or, if we could, at least, try? Sadly, we'll never know, but let me be as clear as I can, if you want to get to the 10th Degree and live the 10th Degree life, being positive all the time is what you have to do.

REMEMBER: PURGE THE NEGATIVITY

Remember, earlier in the book, when we took a ride on our life bus? I mentioned at that time about respect and negativity.

As I said, I have had people in my life that I've fired. They didn't work for me. I've fired friends. People in my life that every time I saw them, they had a complaint. They were whiners. Whether it was the quality of automobile we were selling, or the Canadian economy, or the government, or lousy weather, or the Winnipeg Blue Bombers, or whatever the popular gripe was that day, every time we got together everything was negative. We'd go to a restaurant and the food was terrible or the server was terrible. It just became tiring.

So one day, I looked him in the eye and I said, "Bob, (that's not his name but that's what we'll call him right now), have a nice day, I gotta go." And in the middle of a dinner, I picked up the cheque, paid it on the way out and left.

Well, of course, he called me a few days later. He left me a voice mail and said "Glen, we're all going out to ABC Restaurant, I want you to join us. Can't wait, we're going to watch the game."

I didn't return the call. He sent me an e-mail and said "I haven't heard from you in a while, what's up?" I returned the e-mail, saying, "Bob, come by and see me."

I just can't be around negativity, and so he finally came by the office to see me. He said "Glen? Why aren't you hanging around?" and I said, "Bob, you know that I think truth is important, right?" He said "Yeah, absolutely."

I said "Great, don't force me to tell you why I'm not going to be hanging out with you, I'm simply not going to be hanging out with you anymore."

That was the end of it. I won't have negativity in my life and if you want to get to the 10th Degree, you shouldn't either. I made suggestions, I helped, I tried to give him books to read and he said, "Glen, reading books is crazy. You're just lining publishers pockets." I couldn't believe it. Everything was negative, all the time. I'm sorry, I couldn't help him. He was one of the few people I couldn't lift up. Sometimes, there is just no cure for negativity.

One day, my wife asked me, "Whatever happened to Bob? Why doesn't he come around anymore?" and I had to tell her that no matter how hard I tried, I couldn't get the negativity out of him and I can't have it in my life. There are too many people who depend on me. Three people in particular – my wife and my two sons. But there are also my employees and my close friends. I will not let negativity enter my life; it's not going to happen. Not over and over and over.

THE FIRST STEP

Listen, you don't have to be successful or wealthy or handsome or gifted to get started on the path to the 10th Degree, but you do have to get started on that path in order to get there.

Make the right choices. Start your day with a positive, uplifting reading; decide that you are going to attack your day with a smile, a kind word and a series of kind deeds, stay away from negativity, but be ready to help when it's required of you; and always, always approach your job, your friends, your acquaintances and all the external forces that are thrust upon you with a positive outlook and an open mind.

If you do, you will be well on the way to the 10th Degree.

OUR BEST IDEAS PAGE

A checklist to help you reach Mental Mastery

1. Go to the library and pick up a book. Go to a local bookstore and buy a book. Make sure it's uplifting and positive and remember this: A book is like a playground for your mind.

2. Now I'm not against reading a mystery or classic fiction, but save those books for when you go to bed at night. In the morning

read something inspirational, motivational, positive. Just read it for 15 minutes a day.

3. When you leave for the day – whether you're off to work or school – take the positive message you've read and live it. Attack your day with a smile. After a good workout, a nutritious breakfast and 15 minutes of reading, you should be ready to attack your day.

4. Stay away from newspapers. It's cover-to-cover negativity and nothing good can come from it. Always remember the immortal words of Thomas Jefferson: "A person who does not read a newspaper is infinitely more intelligent and informed than one who does, inasmuch as a person who does not read a newspaper is closer to the truth than one who does."

5. A motivational speaker once said to me, "We exercise daily so we get our physical metabolism working." Here's my message to you: Read something positive daily to get your mental metabolism working.

"Attitude is one of life's key ingredients. Like any ingredient it is a choice of which one you use and don't use. There are only two types of attitude, positive and negative. You choose yours. It's that simple."

- Glen Daman

Book Three

EMOTIONAL MASTERY

We're now getting up early in the morning to have our workout and morning routine is set. We work out, we have a great breakfast and we exercise our mind with a positive, daily reading. Now it's time to master our emotions.

OH, IF OUR HEARTS COULD SPEAK

"Imagine the kind of world we would live in if our hearts could actually speak."

- Glen Daman

THIS ISN'T EASY BUT, OF COURSE, IT'S NOT SUPPOSED BE

When it comes to mastering our lives and reaching the 10th Degree, nothing is more difficult than Emotional Mastery. For most people, mastering of the emotions is overwhelmingly difficult because, in most cases, emotions master them.

Always remember this: The most difficult person you'll ever deal with in your life is you.

You can always read. That's simple. You can just physically get up and make yourself read something inspirational and, with that, you're on your way to Mental Mastery. You can get on a treadmill, walk around your block, do jumping jacks, dance around your house in your underwear or run the staircases at your apartment. You can do all those simple things and you'll be well on your way to reaching Physical Mastery. But Emotional Mastery? This is the toughest assignment you're going to deal with.

Now, in order to take the first step toward Emotional Mastery, let's look back and ask a question: If you're physically ready, and you're mentally ready how is your attitude? Better or worse?

Undoubtedly, if you're physically and mentally healthy, your attitude has to be better. It's certainly better than it was prior to completing our first two steps.

Remember, this is about getting to the 10th Degree. This isn't about maintenance, so we know your attitude is already better than it was. That I can personally guarantee.

So now that your attitude is at the 10th Degree, or at the very least, on its way, Emotional Mastery becomes easier than you might think. There is very little doubt that if your attitude is great, if it's at the 10th Degree, then you are going to be better equipped emotionally to take some of the disappointments, catastrophes or heartaches that face us from time to time. So to begin, being emotionally ready is really nothing more than remembering that the glass is half full, not half empty.

So if you are following the daily steps toward the 10th Degree you have already completed two steps, your attitude is positive and now we have to work on our emotions.

I want you to close your eyes and think about the positive things in your life. That's right, visualize them.

When I close my eyes here is what I focus on: I have a mother and father who love me, I have a wife who is my life partner, who has never left my side through thick and thin, I have two sons who are truly a gift to me. I have a career that I love. With each point I make in my mind, I can visualize each and every one of these people in a friendly, happy time. For example, I'll visualize a romantic dinner with Donna or spending time at the movies, laughing with the boys. Regardless of anything -- and everything -- else that is going on around me, my life is pretty darn good. That positive thinking allows me to chase my goals, and ultimately my dreams, unencumbered by other worries.

People ask me why I go to work every day. I smile and say, "I don't work; I've never worked a day in, well, forever. I love what I do." What would I do on my day off? I'm already doing it.

I've got a home that's amazing, I live in a city that I love, I love the people around me. My friends are the best people on the planet. Imagine if you did this every morning before you started your day. How are you emotionally? Would you feel better about your life? If some of you are reading this and saying "But Glen, I have no positives," well I challenge you. You do have positives. At this stage of your life, those positives may be small, but you can build on them. If you still can't think of any, then I encourage you to see a professional and talk about it, a professional who will be able to help you find the positives in your life that just might be hiding from you.

For the vast majority of us, however, just sit back, take five or 10 minutes and focus on all the positive things in your life.

STEPPING BACK

Whenever and wherever you can, take a step back. It never hurts to just take a breath before responding to a situation. Remember, we've talked about it before, but most of what happens to you in your life is a result of how you respond to external stimuli. And what people do TO you is much more difficult to handle properly than what people do FOR you.

In those stressful situations, the ones in which you would like to say something that you know will hurt you in the morning, just take a deep breath, a step back and as my mother used to say, "Count to 10." I would argue back then, that I still felt the same way. She'd respond by saying: "Keep counting!"

If necessary, don't respond immediately and take a day to think about it. However, I also believe that, most of the time, if you're on your way to the 10th Degree you're going to know how to deal with a tough or adversarial situation almost immediately.

When an extremely difficult situation comes up, whether you've been challenged to a fight, your wife has left, you've just lost a client, whatever that may be, "Don't react to it right away, take a step back."

There's nothing wrong with saying "I don't want to speak about this right now." The key being "right now." I will speak about it. This is an area where I struggle (just ask my wife, Donna) but I'm working on it daily and find that the results are in my favor when I practice this technique.

I'm a firm believer in the theory that if you have a problem you deal with it right away – but you don't react to it right away. There is a difference between reacting and acting. That's why those words are spelled differently. They're two completely different words and, as a result, two completely different responses.

Keep this in mind: When you hear something from a person in a leadership position for the first time, it's likely that your immediate response is to question every word, to think, right away, that your boss or another person on a board or just a colleague at work, is absolutely wrong.

However, the next day – or just the next hour – after you've thought about it and processed it internally, you feel a little different than you did yesterday? Maybe your boss is right. Maybe that is the way to go. Or, maybe your boss is wrong, but after some time thinking about, you come up with a better way to get the job done. So rather than just complaining and being negative, you add to the situation and try to improve upon it in a constructive, as opposed to, a destructive way.

The first step toward Emotional Mastery is to develop the ability to step back. No matter what someone says or does, don't react immediately. Take a breath.

SPEED KILLS

To illustrate the concept of "stepping back," I like to use a story that came to me from one of the many people I meet and work with every day.

Your brother-in-law says to your wife, you are a problem in our family, and your wife calls to tell you that.

You say honey, that's unfortunate. I think we should sit and think about this for a minute or two – or even an hour and a half. Let me respond to you at the end of the day.

Let's say this phone call came to you at work – at, say, 9:00 a.m. You might be ready to get on the telephone and give your brother-in-law a piece of your mind, confront him, put him in his place. You might want to drive down there and confront your brother-in-law face-to-face.

But because you know you want to be a master of your emotions you say, you know what? I'm going to deal with this all morning internally. I'm going to process it. But by 4:30 your thoughts of what you're going to do, will change. You might still want to drive down to his office, but your plan of action is probably going to change. Your response at noon will probably be different than your response at 9:01.

Speed, even in decisions, sometimes kills. So let's take a step back and breathe.

Now, is it possible in all decisions to take a step back before we can react? No, sometimes you have to react to things. Sometimes you don't get the opportunity to choose. The situation forces you to "act" right away. You have to.

At that stage, from your emotional and mental mastery and all the stuff we do at the 10th Degree you will just trust your training and you react properly.

HOW WOULD YOU FEEL IF YOU READ IT IN A NEWSPAPER?

We can't emphasize this enough: You are given choices every day of your life. It's up to you to make the right choices. One way to start making correct choices is to avoid making "emotional" choices.

I know it's not always easy. For instance, when you're angry, you can make angry choices. You can act out, yell at someone or worse yet, strike someone. Violence is never the correct choice, but far too often, if we make emotional choices, we could find ourselves doing things that we would never do if we stepped back and thought deeply and pragmatically about the situation.

You can make sad choices. If what you perceive to be a bad thing happening to you, something that isn't your fault, you might make an emotional choice that isn't healthy.

So here's something to think about. When you're given a choice and you look at the two alternatives pragmatically, not emotionally, what do you see? You probably see a good, safe choice and bad, risky choice. Risk, in and of itself, is not always a bad thing, but always consider this: Regardless of the decision, would you be comfortable with it, if you picked up the newspaper the next morning and read about it.

Would you be happy with your decision? Could you live with it if you read it in a newspaper? If you saw it in the paper would you say, "Oh, I can live with that," or would you say "Oh, my goodness. How could I have done that?"

Ask yourself that question right before you make an emotional decision.

WAKING UP THE NEXT MORNING

I believe that when you wake up the morning after you've had any type of difficult or, yes, even emotional confrontation or conversation with another person, the first thing that comes to mind is regret. If that hasn't come to mind initially, then you have not displayed Emotional Mastery.

At this point I often think of my Grandfather's advice, advice that was given to me when I was getting married. He said, " Never go to bed angry." Take a step back, don't say anything you will regret, but don't go to sleep until you have dealt with the situation with your bride. Reach a point in which you both can agree."

Thanks grandpa, great advice. However, I will admit, I'm far from perfect. There have been a few sleepless nights over the years!

We have many difficult meetings or conversations with employees, employers, loved ones and friends. It's part of every day life. That's why, I often ask myself when I'm having that type of conversation with somebody, "How will I feel about this tomorrow?" I often run that brief, but important question through my head in the middle of a difficult conversation. In fact, I'll often do it before I have the conversation and many times, if I'm not completely confident about how I'll feel about it the next day, I won't have the conversation at all.

We can call that part of reading it in the newspaper, but I'd rather call it this: "Before it even takes place, what does your conscience think will be the result of that conversation the next day?"

If you feel bad about what you said or did – and this is going to be a very, very big part of Relationship Mastery as well – then you are not yet at the 10th Degree. Now, let's be fair. Nobody is perfect. To this day, I'll say things to people – even my wife or mother – that I regret.

When that happens, and it will happen - a 10th Degree person will immediately leave the shower and go to the phone and call his/her mom or employee or friend or he'll wake his wife, and immediately apologize.

"Sweetheart, you know when I told you yesterday that you can go for dinner on your own? I should never have said it and I apologize from the bottom of my heart, and I hope that you have it in your heart to forgive me."

Now, many bosses or supervisors reading this, feel that apologizing to an employee is a sign of weakness. Wrong! I feel it's a sign of leadership. We all make mistakes and it never hurts to show your team that you're human and you can apologize. They will appreciate it and have more respect for you. Is that positive or negative?

Not surprisingly, most of the people I know will say to me, "Boy that sounds corny." But would you rather be cool and have weak relationships? Or corny and have strong relationships and few regrets? Wouldn't you rather be at the 10th Degree? Absolutely. I'd rather be corny and living a 10th Degree life, working every day to master my emotions.

A FATHER-SON STORY

My son said to me not long ago, "Dad, I got a photo radar ticket for $225," and he was really upset about it.

So we sat down and I said "Justin, what emotion are you showing me right now?" And he said "Dad, I'm frustrated and that's the way it is."

So I said, "OK, but lets take a step back." I said "So were you in a car accident?" He said "No, I wasn't." I said "So did anyone get hurt in this car accident you weren't in?" and he said "No, nobody was hurt?" And I said, "So what did you get again?" He said, "I got a speeding ticket by a camera."

I just smiled. "Oh, so were you speeding?"

"Yeah," he said sheepishly. And I said, "So you chose to speed, it was a bad decision and there are consequences for everything we do. Now let me ask you, how much was the ticket for?"

He said, "$225."

I said "Really? I got one today on one of our company cars. It arrived at our address at work and it was for $513. So let me ask you a question Justin: Which would you prefer the $513 ticket or the $225 ticket?"

Not surprisingly he said, "I'll take the $225 ticket." And I said, "So really it's a good day, isn't it? Nobody got hurt, nobody's injured, and you got half the size of the ticket that I got at work today."

He looked at me, shaking his head and I said, "So I think you should buy me lunch." and he laughed and I laughed and he learned a lesson without me losing my temper or without him doing something stupid because he was frustrated and angry because he made a lousy choice.

That's being emotionally ready, it's a bad thing to get a traffic ticket. Nobody likes them and dads sure don't like it when their sons get one. But is it the end of the world? No. We all just have to realize that with every choice we make there are consequences and if we're prepared to pay those consequences, then we should all learn from it.

HANDLING HEARTACHE

"Being told to forget someone you love and move on is like asking someone to reminisce with a person they have never met. Not only is it ridiculous it's impossible."

- Glen Daman

God saw you getting tired,
And a cure was not meant to be.
So he put his arms around you,
And whispered "Come to Me".

With tearful eyes we watched you,
As we saw you pass away.
Although we love you deeply,
We could not make you stay.

Your Golden Heart stopped beating,
Hard working hands at rest.
God broke our hearts to prove to us,
He only takes the Best.

- Unknown

Dealing with death might be one of the toughest things we deal with in our lives. Young or old, when you lose someone you love, it's a loss that can take months, if not years, to get over. For some, it can take decades to move on with their own lives.

There are no words that can change the loss of a loved one. The only thing one can do is focus on the positive memories that you both shared. These memories are forever. As an example, I think about my grandpa Daman every day. We spent so many great times together, times that I re-live and tell my kids about over and over again.

I wrote the following for a friend who lost a family member. She kept saying she missed him beyond words:

"Missing someone is a celebration of their life. It's like having an album of photographs taken of the time spent together. These photographs never fade and are always there, stored in your heart forever."

I've had many people tell me they won't be able to go on and I understand, from my own experience how they feel. But my answer is always, "Yes you will and in fact, you already are." Life moves forward whether we want it to or not. Those around us still depend on us and love us. And that's what will carry us through.

Here is something that might (probably?) have happened to you.

I have a close friend who has had a horrible month. For one thing he's diabetic, so Physical Mastery is always a chore for him. He's had a few problems on the job and just the other day, his wife left him.

Is it terrible? Sure is. Does he have heartache? Yes, he does. Does he need time to heal? You bet.

However, if you're at the 10th Degree and you're emotionally ready for everything that life throws at you, somewhere along the line you can sit down and say, "Wait a minute. I'm still a reasonably healthy guy, I'm still living on this planet and that's a gift. Heck, every day of this life is a gift, I'm not going to worry about what's happened, I'm going to try to learn from this. Because getting better means you have to make mistakes and you learn and move forward."

Sure that sounds impossible right now, but if you have Emotional Mastery, you'll reach the point where you're able to handle it and move on.

So we got together, as friends often do, and I asked him, sincerely, how he was doing. I started by asking him about his two boys who are living with him full time. He smiled and his response was immediate, "Oh, they're awesome," he said.

Then, I said "Wow that's great, but how are you feeling?" and he replied, "I have heartache, I'm lonely and life isn't fair. I've spent 20 plus years with the same woman and now it feels as if it's all for nothing. But other than that I'm feeling better, physically, than ever I have in my life. I've lost 45 pounds. I feel great!"

So I said, "Let me understand this. Your boys are incredible and, physically, you're feeling good. You're healthy and your kids are happy. So, really, life's pretty grand then."

He looked at me, a little confused, and so I continued. "Isn't there a chance you're going to meet someone who's going to sweep you off your feet one day and you'll be so happy you'll think it's the most unbelievable thing that ever happened in your life? I mean, truly, aren't there a lot of wonderful people on this planet? Something tells me you're going to be alright.

"You are a great person. A great dad, great friend, great son. Great people have great things come their way. Sometimes it doesn't happen the way we imagine it will happen, but somehow it still turns out very well."

With that, he looks at me and says, "Wow! You're always positive." And I reply, "Yeah, it kinda sucks to be 10th Degree sometimes."

And with that, we both laughed. It's the 10th Degree. You're emotionally ready, and despite his heartache, he was emotionally ready. He knew that things happen and all we can do is have a good attitude and do our very best. .

As we discussed earlier in this book, our attitude is the key to everything. It's all about steering our life to the 10th Degree.

In a way, it's almost the same as the one thing I make sure to tell people when they buy a car from our company: "It's mechanical, so I can guarantee you it will break. Things manufactured by man will break eventually. So what we do is fix it. Is it breaking all the time? No. Has it broken much at all? No. So let's not focus on the breaking, let's focus on the fact that it broke once in four years and we fixed it. Bad things will happen. To handling the emotional baggage that comes with bad things, we must have a good attitude, think positively and do whatever we can to fix it.

There are some other 12 Step Programs, that claim, "God never sends you something you can't handle," and I agree with that. As long as you are emotionally ready.

There are things that happen in this world that are terrible. When I worked with the Royal Canadian Mounted Police, we attended to suicide calls. That's a terrible thing, one of the saddest things in the world. I look back at those experiences differently now. I think of them this way: Somebody didn't get to those people in time.

Suicide is the most selfish thing a person can do because not only do you take yourself away from people who love you – and no matter how bad you think things are, there are still people who love you – you also leave a great deal of pain behind. And make no mistake, it's very difficult for your friends and loved ones to deal with that pain. However, if you are emotionally ready, you can deal with it.

Someone once said to me, "I don't know if the world will go on," and I just said, "You have no choice. The world will go on without you."

I can personally guarantee that the world doesn't need you or me. It's going to go on. But the people close to you need you. Your family needs you. Your friends need you. No matter how bad you might think it is out there, it's never so bad that you can't deal with it if you are emotionally ready.

A CELEBRATION OF LIFE

"The death of a loved one for many, can be the most devastating thing we face in this journey we call life. It has often been said that there are no words to ease the pain. In many ways I agree with that statement. The only words I try to share are these: Try to use the person who has left us, as a lesson. If he or she taught us or were a role model for us, try to keep those lessons and their wisdom with you and apply them in your everyday life. This would be the biggest compliment to them and the greatest celebration of their life."

- Glen Daman

HOLDING THE LINE

Imagine if you will, your entire world, your being and all the things that accompany your being, have been separated into two different sides by a line.

On top of the line, is a good day, an exciting moment, a positive response from your boss, a kiss from your wife or a gift from your boyfriend, all the things that make you feel good. It's the up.

Below the line, it's unpleasant. This is how you feel when you lose a golf game, miss a deadline, hurt a loved one or forget a task. It's the down.

Holding the Line
Emotional Mastery

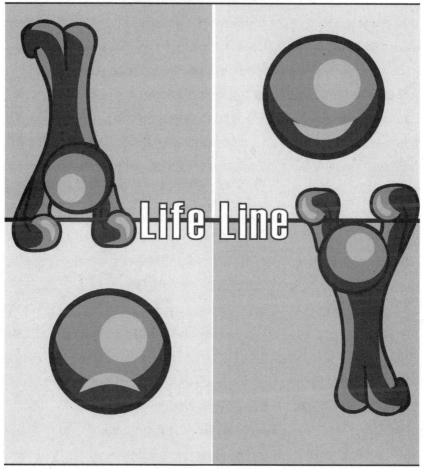

Life Line

Your Center: Never too High, Never too Low - No matter what side your on, you're always Holding the Line.

Now, make no mistake, the ups and downs can be significantly greater – from winning an award, a lottery or a championship to losing a loved one, a job or an appendage. There are highs and lows in our life all the time. From the mundane to the significant, the highs and lows will come and go. The key is not letting the lows get too low or the highs get too high.

That's why we emphasize, "holding the line."

No matter how good something is, or how bad, you can't let the lows get you down or the highs make you believe you are something more than you really are. Oh, it's great to build confidence by having a series of good things happen to you. It also helps build a positive outlook. But you must always keep in mind that we, as a species, are not perfect. There will be bad times to go with all the good. On many occasions those bad situations weren't even caused by us. But there will always be good and bad. You just can't let either reality take control of your life.

Think of your life as a line. It's the middle of the road and you always want to be walking it. It's an old-fashioned clothes line and you always want to be hanging on. Don't lose your handle on the life line and you won't lose your handle on life.

As humans, it's often been said that we are all like manic depressives only a little less manic and a little less depressed. We swing daily from high to low and back to high again. To be successful, to live the 10th Degree life, we have to be careful not let those lows dominate our outlook or those highs change our attitude. We are not invincible. Nor are we losers. We're just people who need to "keep an even keel," as a friend's grandparents used to say.

We need to keep our hands on the life line. If we spend too much time alternating between our personal peaks and valleys, we will not only feel as if we're losing control, but we will appear to others as if we've lost it.

For too many of us, the pendulum of our life never calmly hovers in the middle. It is always swinging from one extreme to another. To live the 10th Degree, we must not let the pendulum swing back and forth. To stop the swinging, we must hang on to the life line.

Too many of us take our successes, ride them to the top and then, inevitably, have the rug pulled out from under us. That's when we slide quickly back to the bottom and we have to claw our way back to the top – if we can ever get there again.

In order to make sure we don't let that happen, in order to continue growing on an even consistent basis, we must maintain a watchful eye on our life line. Take the good with the bad, don't allow ourselves to get too full of our own importance and make sure we never allow the bad things that will inevitably happen to us, drag us into the abyss.

Be calm, be patient and don't get too high or too low. That's a foundation of the 10th Degree life and a great way to live it every day.

ALWAYS THINK POSITIVE

One of the things that is extremely important for all of us to do is to think positive all the time. So every morning do the Emotional Mastery exercise for five or 10 minutes.

Let's do it right now. As I stated above: I have a mother and father who love me, I have a wife who is my life partner, and whom I adore. My two boys have both taught me so much about life and love. I enjoyed what I do. It never feels as if it's work. Who could ask for more?

Sometimes, we still feel down, angry or anxious, later on in the day. I know that happens to me from time to time. So I simply find a spot to be alone for a few minutes and focus on all the positive things in my life again. It's a great way to bring that positive level in your life back to where you need it to be.

Focus on that. Put a smile on your face. In fact, try NOT to smile when you take that inventory. It's difficult, isn't it? I can't frown when I do it.

Close your eyes, focus, and see everything around you. If you do that every day, you'll be able to chase your dreams with a full heart. I don't care if you're 17 or 77 years old.

You close your eyes and say, "This girl in class likes me, I got the best grade that I've ever had on the last math test. My dad's taking me to the ball game on Saturday. Sunday the whole family is going on a picnic. My grandpa and I are building the coolest go-cart of all time." Emotional Mastery is reached when you focus on the positive and the positive becomes your life. As we all know, sometime during the day – every day – we're going to encounter the negative. We can't avoid it. But we also have to approach that encounter with the negative, not with emotion, but with a positive attitude.

OUR BEST IDEAS PAGE

A checklist to help you reach Emotional Mastery

1. Attitude. If you've completed your Physical and Mental Mastery, you already have a good attitude. Now it's about maintaining that attitude when unpleasant things happen. And believe me, unpleasant things will happen to all of us. Take five or ten minutes and focus on the positives in your life. Visualize them.

2. Take a step back. Don't react to the unpleasant things that happen with an emotional response. Take a step back, take a deep breath and think pragmatically before doing or saying something you might regret.

3. We all have choices to make in our lives. Don't make an

emotionally-based choice that you might regret in the morning. Don't let anger or unhappiness unnecessarily influence the correct choices you must make in your life every day.

4. If you make an emotional decision that you regret in an hour, an afternoon or overnight, contact the person you feel you've wronged and apologize immediately. Don't worry about being corny and giving the impression you might be weak. You have one wrong, we all do, make it right.

5. Don't choose to do anything that would embarrass you if you read about it in a newspaper.

6. Don't focus on the unpleasant things that happen. Focus on what you can do to fix the problem. And more importantly, focus on what is right in your life.

Book Four

PROFESSIONAL MASTERY

We've had our workout, enjoyed a great breakfast, done our reading and have a positive mind set for the day and we're prepared to deal with our emotions. Now, it's time to choose the right attitude and head off to meet the world.

HAVE PURPOSE

"When we focus on our goals, it gives us purpose. We can't, however, forget to enjoy the ride. The ride is what our memories are made of. So have a purpose -- and enjoy every step!"

- **Glen Daman**

PROFESSIONAL MASTERY PLANS AND DREAMS

"Living life without dreaming is like a river basin without water, empty and still."

- **Glen Daman**

We have completed our physical mastery, our mental mastery and our emotional mastery. That's done. Now what do we have to do? That's right, you've been paying attention: Next up is Professional mastery.

Attaining Professional Mastery is quite simple: You have to have goals, you have to set those goals and you have to know exactly what it is you're after in your life. It's more than just having a well-paying job. It's about passion. It's about loving every second of your day at work. It's about going to bed at night and you're so excited about your next day at work that it's hard to sleep. Making money is one thing. Being passionate about career is quite another.

That's why you need goals. It's a lot like Alice in Wonderland. When she gets to the fork in the road and says to the Cheshire Cat, "Which road should I take?" And he responds, "Where are you going?" She says, "I don't know." and he replies, "Then it doesn't matter which one you take, does it?"

That's why you must have a plan. Amazingly, there are people who are afraid of this. They are actually scared to have a plan and there are more of them out there than you'd think.

You also have to have a dream. I don't care what that dream is. Dream as big as you possibly can.

I've had a person say to me, "Oh Glen, that's silly." I tell them, "No, it's not silly. It's anything but silly." I tell them, "I don't care what that dream is. You want to have a home on a golf course right beside Tiger Woods? Great!" Now, how are you going to get there?

The first thing you're going to do is set goals for yourself. If you say, "Well I need to have this job or that job." Go get it. "But I work in the mail room and I have to be CEO." Well, then, how are you going to get to CEO? "Well, I have to have a different education." Great! Where do you get that education? "I get it here."

Great. We sit down and start mapping that out. You start at your dream and you work it backwards and set yourself different goals to reach, and you have to reach those goals in order to get to where you want to go. Now, your dream might change! And that's OK, too.

Now those goals should be set regardless of your current situation. So if you say in three years, I need to have $10,000 in the bank, then where will you have to be in a year and a half? In six months? In the next 90 days? 30 days? Next week? Tomorrow?

Now you've broken it down backwards. Now you have daily goals.

That's a big part of Professional Mastery. If you are a Professional Master you will have daily goals and they won't be tasks, they'll be full-blown activities. Tasks, to me, are negative. Activities are something you do to attain your daily goal, which is tied to your weekly goal, which is tied to your monthly goal, which is tied right up to your ultimate goal and then, of course, your dream.

WRITE DOWN YOUR GOALS AND DREAMS:
BE A S.T.A.R.

Now, once you've determined, inside your head, what your goals are going to be, it's time to write them down.

Writing your goals and dreams down on a piece of paper and referring to them on a regular basis is a major step toward Professional Mastery.

Whenever you have written something down on a piece of paper, it's like signing a contract with yourself. You have made a commitment to yourself to follow your dreams by working your goals. It's signed, sealed and delivered and it's up to you to guarantee that the contract is fulfilled.

I love what the great author Dennis Waitley, said: "The reason most people never reach their goals is that they don't define them, learn about them, or even seriously consider them as believable or achievable. Winners can tell you where they are going, what they plan to do along the way, and who will win." I love that quote.

It has often been said that a goal not written down is not a goal. It's a wish. My advice to you is don't wish for Professional Mastery, write down your goals and start the journey toward the 10th Degree. Writing down your goals is a key to reaching them but that won't be enough. Never forget: There is no substitute for action. You must do what you say you will do.

When I work with different groups on reaching their goals, I will often ask them: "Do you want to be a star?" They look at me incredulously and usually respond, "Sure, of course."

Now, when I refer to star I'm speaking about the acronym: S.T.A.R. The S stands for situation. What is the situation? Well, as an example, Tom wants to lose 15 pounds over 6 weeks. T stands for tactic. What is his tactic? For example, he is going to run five kilometres, three times a week, eat right and do yoga once a week. A stands for action. OK, go do it! R stands for result. The result has to be measured.

Tom either he reached his goal or he didn't. If he did not lose 15 pounds after six weeks using the S.T.A.R. chart, what could have been the reason? Well, the situation is not an issue and the result is the result, so the only two variables are either the tactic or the action.

In my experience, having used this model many times in all kinds of situations, the tactic is wrong only 10 to 20 percent of the time and the action, or should I say lack of action, is the problem 80 to 90 per cent of the time. If you write down your goals or if you don't act on your goals, your goals are only wishes.

By definition, Professional Mastery is when we have a dream and we write out our goals on a piece of paper. It's a piece of paper we keep close to us and check every day. Take 15 minutes out of every day to focus on your dream and clearly understand your goals for the day. How long should your daily 15-minute focus time take? That's right. Fifteen minutes. Daily. Simple.

"The pain of discipline hurts less than the pain of regret."
- Unknown

PASSION AND WORK

"Being afraid of failure stops our growth. If you know someone who is successful they will be able to point out more failures in

their life than college degrees on their wall. Failure is an education you can only get from action and effort. Inventors, educators and entrepreneurs would call it experience. I call it real life lessons and failing is a key cog in getting to a 10th Degree life."

- Glen Daman

In order to attain true Professional Mastery, you must enjoy your work, it must make you happy and you have to have the passion that makes it something more than "just a paycheque."

It's one thing for me to continue to tell you to have a great attitude, but if you truly hate your job, you have to move on.

We all have choices in life. Everything we do in our lives is based on our attitude and the choices we make. Remember, you are driving your life bus. If it is parked at the wrong career for eight hours a day, then it's time to change parking lots! If you are miserable in your job and you know that your job is the cause of bad relationships and/or a bad attitude, from morning 'till night, then you must make a change. You can't get to the 10th Degree without a certain degree of legitimate happiness.

How many times have we heard this in a day? "I'm just not happy."

If that's you, you have two alternatives: No. 1 -- and this is the 10th Degree at work -- you can change your attitude toward your job. You can go to work with renewed commitment. Let all the things that your boss does, or your fellow workers do, the things you don't like, let them roll off your back and say, "Live and let live."

You can smile every day, treat people like they were the most important people in the world and pay no attention at all to the negative aura that is part of your daily grind. You can get up early and work out, have a great breakfast and start reading positive and uplifting books and articles that make you happy and give you that all-important emotional boost. You can make the choice that doing your job the way you believe it should be done is more important than worrying about the way your boss can find ways to destroy what you should believe is YOUR work place.

Or No. 2: You can quit.

Now, we all know that in this most recent recession, quitting a job can be an extremely difficult thing to do. We keep hearing about how incredibly tough it is to find work. We keep hearing that if you have a job, no matter how horrible it is, you hold onto it with dear life.

Depending on where you live and what you do, you might just want to look at Plan A and say, "That's exactly what I need to do."

Then again, after giving Plan A a try – and we believe Plan A is a terrific first step, because it IS the 10th Degree – you may find that outside forces have poisoned the atmosphere in which you work. We won't argue that some bosses can be impossible to work for. Some people are just miserable and those people want to transfer their misery to you. We also know that some jobs are simply places to "get a paycheque," every two weeks and provide workers with absolutely no quality of life – or no passion! – for eight or nine hours a day.

If it has reached that stage, then quitting might be the only choice. We know many people who believe that hating their job and then quitting it is a failure, but remember, at some point in the life of every successful person they have failed at something.

You have to weigh the pros and cons of any decision of this magnitude, but it is a choice and if a renewed 10th Degree attitude can't change the abuse that is hurled upon you by a boss who cannot and will not live the 10th Degree, then perhaps it's time to find a new boss.

No doubt, it takes a great deal of confidence and a real commitment to get onto the web, check the job sites, make contact with a headhunter and make a thorough search for available employment. Sometimes, however, these are things you must do to reconcile your professional mastery.

ONE DAY AT A TIME

Today is a new day, a new beginning
It has been given to me as a new gift.
I can either use it or throw it away.
What I do today will affect me tomorrow.
I cannot blame anyone but myself if I do not succeed.
I promise to use this day to the fullest by giving my best, realizing it can never come back again.
This is my life and I choose to make it a success.

- Unknown

Indeed, every day is a gift and what you do today will affect your life – and other people's lives – tomorrow.

So one important thing you need to do is turn the rest of your life into one day at a time. Because if you failed yesterday, could you adjust that failure the next day? I think you can. I think we all can. But you can't do anything tomorrow unless you've done all you can today.

Say I'm in sales and yesterday, I was short three phone calls. Could you add three calls today? Probably. Heck, if you got up and did your Physical Mastery and your Mental Mastery, you could probably get those three phone calls done by 9 a.m.

If nothing else, you could add one call today, one tomorrow and one the next day. At that point, you've caught up. The failure – and failure is personal – is now nothing. It's completely forgotten.

Of course, the same thing can be said for everything. If you know that you didn't do your 30-minute workout and only did 25 minutes, you could do five more tomorrow. That's what happens when you maintain a daily focus. Keep it one day at a time. Do it and you'll be a Professional Master.

By the way, I don't care what you do. If you push a broom, if you sell insurance, if you're a sportscaster or a company president, if you are physically better, if you are ready, if you are mentally better, if you are emotionally better and you know what your activities are for that day, you will be a Master. And if you were ready every single day to have the best day you could possibly have, how do you think that would affect your relationships at work?

I can pretty much guarantee that they would improve dramatically.

WHO DO YOU WANT TO BE?

Now, this should bring us to Relationship Mastery, but first I want you to see how this all builds. In the first three steps – Physical, Mental and Emotional Mastery – you are taking care of you. In the fourth step – Professional Mastery – you take care of the company you work for or the company you own. You also take care of the people around you in the office, because with your great attitude you're known as the guy in the office who is always positive and always great to be around. When I speak to groups or sales teams, I always ask which guy do you want to be?

Do you want to be this guy? "Oh, it's raining. It's raining today. We're not going to have any business at all, there's no water in the water cooler. Nobody ever cares about us or the water cooler. I don't know about you, but if there was a better job, I'd be gone."

Does that sound familiar? Sure, in millions and millions of offices there is a guy who moans and groans and whines and cries all the time. Nothing but negativity all the time. I don't want to hang with that guy, but who knows, maybe you do.

I want to hang with this guy: "Morning boys, what's up this morning? Give me a high-five. Did you see my Leafs last night? Blew up again. Are you kidding me? Unbelievable. I notice there's no water in the water cooler, but until the guy comes in to replace the bottle, I brought a couple of bottles of water from home. They're in the fridge, help yourself. What's going on folks? Are you all ready for today?"

Which guy would you rather work with? The guy whose happy, ready to get it on, ready to help, ready to make you happy or the guy who hates everything, and spends the morning whining, not working.

Now look, I'm not naïve. I know there are all sorts of people who just feed off the negativity. But if everyone got on the The 10th Degree program, what a world we'd live in!

When I spoke to a group last year and used that previous example, I asked them, which guy would you rather work with? The second one? Right. Then I said, "Imagine if all of you actually believed that, because I figure some don't. You probably shut me out at "good morning." For all those people who really believe they'd rather work with the second guy, I have another question for you: Which guy or gal would you rather be? The second one, again? Great, so do it!

It's simple. You can own this book for $24.99. There's a plug.

And remember, you don't need a master's degree, you don't need a degree at all. Heck, you don't even need a high school education to be a positive person. This stuff is simple and I'm the poster boy for simple. Believe me, if it was hard I couldn't have done it.

Remember, as I told you before, I have a high school diploma. I don't have a university degree. So if people out there are suggesting, "Oh you have to be special," they aren't even close to the truth. You don't have to be special at all. Just positive. That's all it is. It's really simple.

Professional Mastery begins by having clear, defined, written goals. Then you focus on them every single day. That's every single day. I can't possibly start to list every single profession or vocation or career out there, I can't even begin, but I don't care what you do for a living, you can set personal, professional goals for yourself.

And it doesn't matter how old you are. Remember, we all choose our attitude. It is a choice. Simple as that.

People who have heard me speak often send me e-mails, great e-mails. I love every one of those the e-mails.

The positive ones are just amazing, I've had people who are 60 years old say, "Glen, it's been two years since I've seen you and yet I've done more and grown more in those two years than I did in my first 58. I've put more money in the bank in the past two years than I did in the previous 30 years of working."

This stuff is simple, that's why it works.

OUR BEST IDEAS PAGE

A checklist to help you reach Professional Mastery

1. Dream big. Have a dream and write it down. You can change it any time you like, but have a dream.

2. Set goals. Then set up a plan that helps you achieve those goals. Write down your goals with a clear time line that you can meet, a time line that enables you to reach those goals.

3. Make the changes you need to make to achieve the goals you've written down. If you need more education, find a way to get more education. If you need to change jobs, get out and do it. Do what you need to achieve your goals and reach your dream. Action is the engine that drives us to our goals.

4. Attitude. If you've completed your Physical, Mental and Emotional Mastery, you already have a great attitude. Now it's about maintaining that attitude when you go to work and complete your activities, not tasks, every day.

5. Have passion, Love your job. And if you don't love it, get a new one. You're at your job eight or nine hours a day, love it or leave it. Approach every day with a great attitude and passion for what you do.

6. Spend 15 minutes each day focusing on your written goals and dreams. Make sure you know, every day, what you need to do to get closer to your dream.

Book Five

RELATIONSHIP MASTERY

You're in shape, you eat right, you read to lead and you have a great attitude. All that's left is to learn how to use your tools to create great relationships with everyone you come in contact with every single day.

YOU GET WHAT YOU GIVE

"The level of love we feel is determined by the level of love we give. Unselfish love we give to family, friends and even strangers. This gives us a feeling of true happiness. The level of this is dependent on how many days in our lives we give love. The happiness we feel is like a reflective ray from the sun and it will light up the darkness that tries to shadow our love."

- Glen Daman

RELATIONSHIP MASTERY

"My key motivation is love. My religion is kindness."

- The Dalai Lama

Here's something you've probably heard before: "We take relationships for granted." Think about it. We do.

I don't care if it's your parents, siblings, friends, spouse, girlfriend, boyfriend, whomever, wouldn't it be very cool if everyone on the planet had the same relationship thought process as a Labrador Retriever? Seriously. Can you imagine what the world would be like?

I have a Chocolate Lab. I can pretty much guarantee that she doesn't care if I have a big zit on my nose or if my breath is bad. She doesn't care if I put on the wrong tie with the wrong-colored shirt. She doesn't care if I failed at the office that day. She doesn't care if I got a speeding ticket. Fact is, she doesn't care about anything at all. She just knows that she loves me and she will be loyal to me no matter what. And she also knows that I love her and she appreciates it every minute of every day.

When she greets me, she acts like it's the greatest moment in her life.

Wouldn't it be great if all of our relationships were like that? Is that Utopian? Yes. Is it possible? Absolutely not. But wouldn't it be cool if everyone tried to achieve that? Understanding, of course, that we'd never actually get there.

Trouble is, relationships are the number one, most important things on this planet.

And make no mistake, Relationship Mastery is not only important with our close, inner circle of friends and family, but it is the most important thing we face every day with everyone we come near or everyone we touch.

Tenth Degree Relationship Mastery means that when you meet someone, whether they are close to you or simply a stranger, you leave that person feeling uplifted, feeling better than he or she did before they met with you.

Every meeting you have, every day of the week, should either reinforce the other person's or persons' positive attitude and enthusiasm, or give them hope when they feel there is none and/or confidence when they absolutely need it. That's it. That's Relationship Mastery. It's about making the people you come in contact with feel better about themselves and the world around them, no matter the level of despair or hatred they felt about anything, before they came in contact with you.

Whether that interaction is with a co-worker, a friend, a classmate who is bullied, a stranger you sit beside in the airport, a person with special needs, a player you coach or the person you love, if you have Mastered Relationships, then you are the shoulder to cry on, you are the coach who makes a player better, you are the father/mother who gives self-esteem to his or her children and you are the husband/

wife, the man/woman, who brings love and light to your wife or partner.

I believe that every encounter we have with another man, woman or child is just another opportunity to make a difference in the world.

I believe that if each of us strives to Relationship Mastery with every person with whom we come in contact, we can change the thinking, the actions and the attitudes of entire communities, our nation and ultimately the world. And yes, we can do it, one interaction at a time.

And let me also tell you this: If you can Master your Relationships, then everything else in life will be so easy, you'll be blown away.

OK, so the next question is: How do we get there? How do we reach Relationship Mastery?

Come with me on a journey.

GIVE MORE THAN YOU TAKE

"You need to give to get. Giving begins the receiving process."
- Robin Sharma

If you have a positive outlook, you've taken Step 1. If you really, truly give more than you take, I don't mean that monetarily, but emotionally with people around you, then you're on your way toward Step 2 in our trek toward Relationship Mastery.

I always joke, if your spouse is putting away three of the five dishes, then you make sure you walk the dog more often than he or she does.

We all have to give and take to help each other out in a relationship, but whether it's a spouse or a friend, my goal is to always leave people feeling like they got something from me. Doesn't have to be a lot. Maybe it was just a smile or a ride to the store. Maybe you held the door open for a stranger. Something. Give more than you take and your relationships will be off on solid footing.

Remember that relationships are the most important things we'll ever have because, really, why are we on this planet otherwise? You can have all the money in the world, but if you don't have some kind of relationship with another human being, you're emotionally bankrupt. A person who dies with a million friends is wealthier in many ways than a person who dies with a million dollars.

One of my favourite quotes came from a pig farmer I knew growing up who said to me, "Glen, you can have all the money in the world, but money is over-rated. Pigs won't even eat it. And they'll eat anything."

Now is there anything wrong with having a lot of money? No! But be generous with people and by that I mean, have strong relationships with people. Having a friend is having someone who will stand in front of any danger for you and not worry about the consequences. He'll push you out of the way of the bus, not put you under it. For those hockey fans out there he's the one who will take the hit along the boards to chip the puck out.

And you'll do the same for him. That's a relationship.

Without positive relationships – or at least one positive relationship – we would live in a very lonely world, and loneliness might be the second worst thing in the world.

Of course, the first rule you must understand going in, is this: If you have a chip on your shoulder, going into a relationship – if you intend to take more out than you're prepared to give -- then you'll have a big problem. If you enjoy being with somebody, anybody, and you cherish that time together - knowing you can never get it back – you must enjoy it. And in order to truly enjoy it, you must give more than you can take

Once you've decided, in your own mind, to make a commitment to a relationship, whether it's a client or your spouse, you have to go into it believing you are going to put more into it than you receive from it. And, hopefully, the other person in the relationship believes the same thing. Then you have the perfect balance of give and take.

That's the game plan. That's what's in the play book. If you're a 10th Degree person, that's the offense you run.

MY GREATEST JOY IN LIFE: ELEVATING THE PERSON ACROSS FROM ME

During one of our training sessions, I was asked; "What is your greatest joy?" It was a great question and I had a very simple answer: "Knowing that I've elevated the person across from me. If I can elevate every single person I interact with, whether it's for one minute, one hour, one day, one week or one year, I've given something important to that relationship.

There was an interesting proverb I learned once: It said, "If I could leave the earth, better than I found it, then I'd be happy. Then I've accomplished something." I've never forgotten that.

DO YOU WANT TO BE RIGHT, OR DO YOU WANT TO WIN?

That's something I always say to my staff: "Do you want to be right? Or do you want to win?" Because in theory, saying that we should both give 50 per cent to a relationship, is probably fair and balanced. If we're friends, that's probably right. But do you want to be right or do you want to win? I think winning means that the person across from you has respect and love for you, you have that for them, your relationship is insanely strong, incredibly strong, you're loyal to each other and if that means you have to give more to the other person then that's OK. You've won.

Here's another example: You purchase a new car but you sense that the person you bought it from was not being forthright with all the details. How do you deal with that type of interaction?

The first question I always ask is: "What was the goal?" Was the goal, in this case, just to buy the particular car you wanted at the best price? Or did you want to buy a car, service it at the dealership and continue the business relationship with the person at that dealership? If your goal was the latter, then don't buy the car. This way, you avoid confrontation in the future with a person you already did not trust. They didn't sell a car, you didn't make an enemy so you win.

I had something similar to that, happen to me at my last dealership. My goal was to get more stock, but a representative from the company told me it was impossible to get more stock. I didn't understand why and did a little investigating. I found out that the manager got so upset at this rep that he got angry and together, they wrecked the relationship with the dealership.

Now, I had just taken over and I needed stock. I had to figure out something that would help rebuild the relationship. So I spoke to the representative again and he told me: "You aren't getting stock because you people screwed up.

"Hmmm," I thought. I knew for a fact that we didn't screw up. That's because I had all the data and those numbers don't lie. I knew we hadn't "screwed up," but for me, winning was a lot more important than being right. So, I said, "You know what? Thank you for pointing that out and I'd really like to use your expertise, your knowledge – because you're the guy who knows how to solve my problem – to help me get this place in better shape, so those errors don't happen again." Magically, from the big car tree, some automobiles fell right into our dealership.

Was it right? No. We hadn't done anything wrong. As a matter of fact they screwed up, big time. But the rep's insecurities came into play for him and so I just agreed with him. That's what he was after. He wanted me to agree that we'd screwed up.

Now, I had another manager who said, "Glen, that's wrong and you know it." And I said to him, exactly what I always say, "Do you want to be right or do you want to win?" And that's why I always ask, when it comes to any relationship, "What's the goal?"

REMEMBER: DON'T WALLOW IN NEGATIVITY

We've talked from the beginning of the program about having negativity in our lives. It can't be there. It's as simple as that. The fastest way to get to the 10th Degree is to completely purge the negativity in your life. Get rid of it, anyway you can.

Now, look, I'll be the first to admit that there are times when there will be negativity. People have problems. But I'll help you, as best I can, to solve those problems. You don't have to dwell on it and I won't.

Let me give you another example: I had a guy phone me one time. He said, "Glen, I've heard you speak a couple of times and I have to ask you a question." I said "Sure, what's that?" He said, "You can always fix it. But I have a big, big problem. I work for a guy, and this is how I make my living, and he's my supervisor, and he ruins my day at hello."

My first response was probably too simple, I said, "What you do is you try and get him into a 10th Degree life," and of course, he said, "Sorry Glen, that's not possible."

So, I said, "Have you tried?" He said, "Well, no," and I said, "Do yourself a favor and try." I convinced him to just give it a shot and work with this guy. Try to help him be a little less negative."

Well, not surprisingly, he phoned me back about 60 days later and said, "Ah, Glen, it didn't work."

"Didn't work?" I said.

"Yeah," he replied. "What should I do now?"

I said "Quit." He said "I can't quit." I said "Why not?" He said, "This is how I make my living?" I said, "Really? Are you not employable anywhere else? You don't have the skills? You don't believe in yourself?

As Og Mandino says in his book, *The Greatest Salesman in the World*: "You're nature's greatest miracle, do not let it end with your birth. Get out there and do something else."

But he was in a comfort zone, and because we don't like the fear zone, we'd rather be comfortable wallowing in negativity every day.

So fast forward the movie, I'm proud to say, he eventually did quit. Fast forward again, he's now a manager in another business that's in the same kind of industry, happier than he can believe, and he and his wife are in a different house, a bigger house, their lives are amazing. All because there are times when relationships break down and the only cure for negativity is to get away from it.

Now remember, getting a bigger house and/or accumulating more money are not the biggest victories. For my friend, his happiness and the happiness of the people around him, were the greatest rewards of all.

Now I know, from the many training sessions I've given, that there are a lot of people out there who think, "Glen, you can't make everyone out there positive, stop living in a Utopian world." It's true.

And let's not forget, many of you reading this may be that negative person, so work on yourself first and you'll be amazed at how everyone around you "gets better." As a sales trainer, Jackie Cooper has been quoted as saying "Do a check up from the neck up."

By the way, just for the record, I am not naïve enough to believe that everyone reading this book will change. But we can always have faith.

Because you know as well as I do that there are people who just get off on the negative and for the most part, you shouldn't have to do anything as drastic as fire a friend. Then again, sometimes you DO have to fire a friend. And if you're a manager and you have a negative performer in your company, you just might have to ask them to leave. Let me show you what I mean.

And this is a true story. A good friend of mine owns an automobile dealership. He has an employee who just so happens to be the best sales person at the dealership, but he's an extremely negative guy. So I asked my friend, how many sales people do you have? He said, "Seven sales people and this guy I'm having trouble with is the best salesperson on the floor. Everybody else sells X number of cars and he sells three times as many."

So I said to my friend, "What if I told you that this guy's negativity is what's holding back your other sales people?" He drives the rest of your staff to distraction and in order for everybody else to improve, you have to let him go."

My friend was shocked. He said, "Glen, I can't do that, he sells too many cars." So I said, "You know you're not going to fix your problem then are you? You've already gone through the exercise of trying to help this gentleman out with his negativity and his lousy attitude. If you don't get him off your floor, you might just as well fire everybody else."

It took awhile, but my friend finally reached his limit and he let Mr. Negative go. Six months later, three of the people who were left had tripled their numbers, one other salesperson had doubled his, and another had a slight increase. So, in the end, with a happy staff, my friend's dealership was actually selling more cars.

Because sometimes, in order to foster the best relationships, you have to get the poisoned attitude out of the room.

Making sure the people around you have good relationships, is a big part of Relationship Mastery.

THE IMPORTANCE OF FRIENDS

As you have already read, I grew up poor. As a result, I have often been asked by people who have had similar situations to mine: "How did you get through some of those really tough times while you were growing up."

I always answer the question the same way. With one word: Friends. I simply would not be where I am today without some of the best friends anyone could ever wish for. I know I was fortunate. Many of the people I've spoken with not only went through what I did, but they did it in even worse circumstances and they did it with no friends at all. I have to admit, when I was young, I don't think I would have been that strong.

Parents, I encourage you to get your sons and daughters involved in school groups, after-school groups or sports teams – and as soon as possible – in order to help them get contacts and cultivate healthy relationships. Make no mistake; this is one of the keys to a The 10th Degree life. In fact, it could be the difference between life and death. Young people need to know others do care; they need to know people from outside their immediate family who truly love them.

There were many people who were friends of mine who helped me achieve what I've achieved. Some of those people helped me while I was growing up, others while I was just getting started in business and yet others who still help me out to today.

While the friends I have today are precious to me, I want to especially point out the ones from my early days who helped me every day when I lived with my family in that trailer. Guys – and girls – such as Uriah, Kyle, Greg, Joanne and Jeff, just to name a few. However, I must say a special thank you to...

Mark Pelletier: I still have a hard time referring to Mark as a friend. He is the one guy who I actually cut fingers with and declared my blood brother (Yeah, you're right, I saw it in a movie). We took it seriously and to this day I refer to him as my brother. He was with me every step of the way from the time I was five-years-old. He saw the tears of joy and sadness. He was the best man at my wedding and I at his. He is the only human being who knows every story in detail. I still talk to him almost every single day.

David Stott: My official "best" friend. Dave brought me home for a weekend sleepover during a rough patch back at the trailer and we joke, I left 10 years later. Dave's parents Gary and Doris or "Mom and Pops," as I refer to them, have also played an important role in my success and are still a big part of my life. The Stott home has always been like a second home to me.

Brett Hachkowski: "Moose," as I call him, was incredible. He was the one guy to stick with me during a very turbulent time in my life, when political peer pressure in high school made my life very difficult. I will never forget him or his parents Tony and Judy (another Mom). I always felt extremely comfortable in their home and I ate almost every lunch there. I still owe you! They live in Pennsylvania now and even though I don't see them or talk to them much, I think of them often.

YOUR BEST FRIEND

Once you meet your best friend, your life will change forever.

You give up a part of your heart and you will be together in spirit for as long as you live.

No matter how long you are apart, you will pick up where you left off, as if life simply has a pause button.

You laugh from your belly, smile 'till it hurts and hug to be one.

When you are confused, worried or frightened, all you have to do is call, or simply think of each other, to get back to, "I'm OK."

When together you always feel safe, truly happy and vibrant, ready to make every situation the 10th Degree.

Your best friend always supports your dreams and makes them seem within reach.

This is the only person who will ever know all of your weaknesses and hear of all your defeats, but they do not judge, rather they love you more simply by anticipating your next victory in life.

They know the true you and that's why they are there.

Finding your best friend is the greatest gift life can give us.

ON LOVE

If you are blessed enough to find the one you love and want to spend the rest of your life with that individual then you are, simply, the richest person in the world.

It's an advantage to have this gift, an advantage in life that many wished they had. Be thankful for your life partner and hold onto your partner with all of your being.

I had a great conversation with a dear friend one day and said if most people paid as much attention and cared for their spouse and the relationship with that person as much as they do on their career or their hobbies, the divorce rate would drop at an alarming rate. Family lawyers would close up shop.

This friend is in the home renovation business and we used the metaphor of a house like that of a couple. All the rooms in the house are all the things we face in the world, living room is the career, kitchen is the kids, and bathrooms are the finances on so on. Meanwhile, the master bedroom is the couple and their relationship. Far too often couples pay attention to all the other rooms. They remodel them, clean them constantly, update, change the décor, all the while ignoring their own room. After all, no one sees that room. Then, one day they wake up and its time to remodel that room, but now it's too late, they don't feel the same way anymore. They don't want to make the effort. They start to feel like guests in that room. They're no longer comfortable and they sell the house.

It was a great analogy and has always stuck in my mind. If we all agree that true love is a gift that most would give anything for, then why is it that those of us who have it take it for granted? Same reason we take our health for granted. We don't think it will ever be taken away and we all know that this is simply not true. Love is not just a feeling on its own. It needs attention and maintenance just like the fragile flower that often represents it, the rose.

True love goes well beyond physical attraction. Love is built or broken with every word spoken, every smile given. Our arms can let go, but our heart cannot. We will never settle until we find true love. Again it is a gift, so when you find it care for it like the precious thing it is.

Now, I certainly understand that many of you are reading this and probably saying, "I agree but how?" Here's how:

Attention and maintenance of a loving relationship doesn't have to be expensive. It can, if you like, but it doesn't have to be. If you have the financial resources here are some great ideas:

1. Do lunch, minimum once a week, together. You take your clients to lunch, treat your wife to a nice lunch four times a month.
2. Candle light dinner at an upscale restaurant minimum once a month.
3. Buy her a dozen roses, or the flowers she loves, every week, not just at Christmas or anniversaries or Valentine's Day.
4. Send her a love card every day.

Now, if its not in the budget how about:

1. Handwritten sticky notes around the house that have love sayings on them.
2. Send her a love letter via email or a text a couple times a week.
3. A simple voice mail saying how much you love him/her and it can be sensual or "spicy," will bring a smile to your partner's face.

My point in all of this is to keep your relationship like it was when it started, for some of us that could be years ago. Or, if you are just starting out and you do this already, KEEP IT UP.

Now you ask me for how long? The answer is simple: Forever.

I WISH

"I miss you when we are apart and can't get enough of you when we are together. You are my earth angel, my life's gift. And I know you are a gift many never receive. The love I feel for you has no definition, no explanation. My wish is that you could see yourself through my eyes, hear your voice with my ears, hold you with my arms and kiss you with my lips. Then I would have the joy of sharing this feeling with you. Forever is not a word it's a place. A place where the sun can be turned off as our love shines bright enough to light up our existence."

- Glen Daman

BELLY LOVE

"If you can maintain belly love with someone, you have accomplished relationship mastery. There are many people who will never achieve that."

- Glen Daman

Do you have a person in your life that you can tell absolutely anything to and you never have to worry that it will "get out?"

Think about it, you can tell someone your deepest personal secrets with no worry, no thought that the person you trust would ever betray that trust. And it could be any secret, no matter how big or small. This is the person you tell your true feelings to or your real opinions to, even if they are not the popular opinions of the day or if the feelings you have would not be acceptable to others.

Belly Love is a title I give to true love that is directed at someone you hold with the ultimate trust. There might be more than one of these people in your life, but it's likely a very small group.

Granted, there are many of us who might not have anyone in this special category. Most of us trust to a point, but belly love has no boundaries.

Now, you might assume the person closest to you is a spouse and if it is your spouse, congratulations. However, for many people, their closest friend, ally and trusted soul mate is not their partner. You see, this love is not necessarily tied to a physical relationship. That's right, it's not necessarily sexual.

Why do I call it belly love? Actually, the answer is simple. As you know, I grew up in rural Manitoba, Canada and animals in the wilderness, when they're being attacked by predators, will instinctively protect their under belly. After all, it is a pretty vulnerable spot. The ultimate trust any animal will display is when they bare their underbelly. It's a pretty clear sign. It shows that they don't feel threatened.

I always think of the different domesticated dogs we had in our farmyard while I was growing up. One, specifically, was named Queeny, our female German Shepard. She was a great guard dog and some would say, she was even quite mean. But, I remember playing with Queeny when I was a 10-year-old and she was rolling on her back with me rubbing her belly. She trusted me totally. She knew I would never hurt her and, at the same time, I knew she wouldn't hurt me.

When you trust someone with your life that is the ultimate trust and, by "life" that can also mean your reputation, career, family or your physical health. I'm blessed to have people with whom to share belly love.

My hope is that you have or will find a love this true, as well.

A 30-DAY BOOK OF READINGS

I believe that anytime we grow or become more educated about life, or ourselves, or the people we love, there is a price to pay. That price can be monetary or even physical – like muscle pain or the feeling of loneliness or heartache.

There is a payment required for growth no matter what. Staying together as we grow personally and as a couple is, at times, a challenge because love isn't just a feeling, but also a decision for us both.

Love isn't perfect and often the fairytale romance is an unrealistic carrot that is put in front of us and chased until we tire out. Reality is, love doesn't come easy. Love requires getting over obstacles, facing challenges, staying silent when we want to speak or speaking when we want to stay silent.

Love means being committed to never letting go. Love is work, however realizing that every second of it, every minute and every day is worth it because you choose to do it together as one joined by your hearts.

We all need to be reminded at times that love is not just a word. It is the ultimate sacrifice to one another – forever.

That is true love. The 10th Degree love.

Back at the start of our journey, when we started on the road to Mental Mastery, I asked you to read something inspirational or uplifting every day.

I'm sure you've been doing that. After all, we're almost finished

Book 5 and, therefore, I assume we're on the verge of The 10th Degree.

However, just in case you've run out of inspirational readings, I'll fix you up. Over the next few pages, I will give you a daily passage to read. This daily passage will give you something uplifting directly from our teachings in Relationship Mastery.

Read one per day for the next 30 days and then come back and re-read your favourites. This is a great way to get a firm grasp on Relationship Mastery as well as adding to the reading portion of your day in Mental Mastery.

DAY 1

Meeting someone is fate, being friends is a decision that is made, falling in love is beyond anyone's control.

DAY 2

Remember this could be the last time you say goodbye, goodnight. So make it count. Hug longer, squeeze tighter and never forget to say I love you.

DAY 3

There are so many factors involved in healthy relationships. The ability to communicate effectively is one of the most important. The route to mutual satisfaction within any relationship depends on it. There are two ways to communicate with others: effectively and ineffectively. Be effective.

DAY 4

I've never seen a smile that is not beautiful. It is the only place the light can escape from our heart.

DAY 5

Fate introduced us. Love made us who we are together.

DAY 6

You are my spirit in the human form, a friend I can never replace.

DAY 7

The relationship that we share is like a fork in the road: We go our separate ways but always end up together. The love shared is in the purest of forms. It feels like we can share all and communicate without the necessity of words, yet no time spent together is long enough to satisfy.

DAY 8

I always knew you were my friend, but I'm still in awe that you are my angel.

DAY 9

Every word we speak is the opportunity to make a conversation, lift a person's feelings, or improve a group's day, either bad or good.

We as humans are the only beings with this gift, so choose your words wisely.

DAY 10

We often don't reveal our true feelings. Sometimes the message we send is not clear. If our heart had the ability to speak would our world be a different place?

DAY 11

You should never hold anyone in your arms that you don't already hold in your heart.

DAY 12

There is only one thing that frees us from all strife and pain. That one thing is love.

DAY 13

A person's arms can pick you up, but their words can elevate you to a new level.

DAY 14

If you knew that the moment you were currently living in would create a powerful memory, would you savor it more?

DAY 15

Life is full of change. Amidst all the change around us, some things are by the day, even by the hour, only one thing is constant.

That one thing is my love.

DAY 16

Missing someone is a celebration. It's like having an album of photographs taken of the pure love spent together. These photographs never fade and are always there, stored in our heart.

DAY 17

When our mind and heart disagree, we can never be truly happy. We must follow one and lead the other.

DAY 18

True love is beyond physical attraction. It is something that is not controlled. This love grows with every word spoken, every smile given. True love is a feeling and it is not controlled by anything. It's a true act of nature. Our arms can let go but our heart cannot. We will never settle until we find true love.

DAY 19

The moisture from your lips is the nourishment for my heart.

DAY 20

You know true love when you feel like you've been together your entire life, but it's not long enough to satisfy your heart.

DAY 21

Being told to forget someone you love and move on is like asking someone to reminisce with a person they have never met. Not only is it ridiculous it's impossible.

DAY 22

Sometimes perfect relationships are held back by not so perfect situations.

DAY 23

Missing someone happens when our body and our heart are in two different places.

DAY 24

When you experience the pain of loss, whether it's a friend, family member or significant other, find comfort in knowing that the common thread in all of them is love. The kind of love that is stored forever in your heart. Even though they have left our ground they will rest forever in our hearts never to leave again.

DAY 25

A smile is our natural way to light up the world. A hug is the handshake of love. We could all make a difference if we smile more often and hug longer.

DAY 26

Remember, physical and mental mastery is all about starting our metabolism.

DAY 27

We may be separated by many kilometers, but never really apart, for friendship is not gauged by distance but by the heart.

DAY 28

Friendship, like any relationship, should feel like a privilege. Being together should raise the level of both people's lives, each taking great strides to improve and strengthen daily.

DAY 29

Your ratio of beauty inside to out is truly remarkable. I think of you when I read Butler's quote: "Optimism is essential to achievement and it is also the foundation of courage and true progress." Your progress is amazing in such a short time. Like the old Mexican proverb states "no fate is worse than a life without a love."

DAY 30

People who find true happiness in life aren't necessarily the ones with material wealth. They are the ones who have relationship wealth. Their inner circle is the purest of unconditional love. These people, on a daily basis make the most of what comes their way. They know that the present day is a gift, never leaving a word unsaid and they always squeeze every last drop out of every moment together. The secret to the brightest future is in the foundation of these relationships. Also, the understanding that while we gain knowledge from the past and present, we cannot move forward unless we release the weight of today's heartache. If we master the art of letting go daily, we will never carry this weight from the past and we will fly high above those with struggle. Leading us to the 10th Degree.

OUR BEST IDEAS PAGE

1. Always leave the people in your life feeling better about themselves. To reach the 10th Degree Relationship Mastery, you must concentrate on lifting up the person across from you.
2. Always give more than you take.
3. In all relationships, it's more important to win than to be right.
4. Purge the negativity.
5. Remember: Love means being committed to never letting go. Love is work, however realizing that every second of it, every minute and every day is worth it because you choose to do it together as one joined by your hearts.
6. If we continue with our Physical Mastery and continue with our Mental Mastery by reading more and more each day, then we should be healthy enough and in the right frame of mind to reach

Relationship Mastery. In fact, Physical Mastery can be something as simple as going for a walk with a loved one. You can always talk about Relationship Mastery and Physical Mastery at the same time. There is certainly nothing wrong with doubling up on these things.

WELCOME TO THE 10TH DEGREE

Five things to remember in order to live the 10th Degree:

1. Don't hold a grudge and never hate.
2. Deal with issues immediately but without emotion. Never sleep on them.
3. Live within your means.
4. Give more than you take.
5. Take time to listen to those you love.

WRAPPING UP

Thanks for coming on our journey. For me, the 10th Degree never gets old. It is, indeed, a way of life. Our attitude, our approach to every day, our love and respect for each other and our mastery of the mental, physical, emotional and professional, plus all of our relationships is worth working at – hard – every single moment of our lives.

Remember, your journey did not bring you to Level 4 or 5. This isn't some half-cocked, do-you-what-you-can-do, fake-it-till-you-make-it race to some mediocre level of self-esteem. This is a program, that if done as outlined, will give you – and, in many ways, the people around you – a new life. If you do the steps, you will reach the 10th Degree and you will remain there forever – just so long as you keep doing the steps. Every day.

One hour a day. That's all I ask. Just one hour a day and your life can be rich, rewarding and full of love. You have the choice. You decided your attitude and the approach you will take to whatever life throws at you. Remember, we don't always get to choose what happens to us. Often, we have no control over the external forces that come at us every day, but we do have the choice on how we react to those external forces. Face them with confidence, with intelligence, with thought and with a positive attitude and the things we believe are problems will disappear before we know it.

Live life that way, and you will live a 10th Degree life.

However, before we turn the 10th Degree over to you, we have one more game to play. A friend of mine, we'll call her "Jennifer" has been going through some difficult times. Like most of us, she frets, loses sleep, gets down on herself and wonders, "What's the point?" She knows she should know better. She knows that attitude is a choice and relationships must be nourished every day, but like many of us, she'll find herself in a rut, a rut that she just can't shake.

One day, I asked her to play the Big Rock Game... it opened her eyes, her mind and her heart.

LET'S PLAY THE BIG ROCK GAME

It was just one of those days.

Now my friend Jennifer is pretty and smart and loved. She has everything going for her, good looks, a college education, nice job, great family and a boyfriend who treats her with honour and respect. For Jennifer, life is good.

At least, life appears to be good. That is, if you don't happen to be Jennifer.

Jennifer, it seems, always has a problem. Some of her friends just shrug it off and refer to her as "the office drama queen," but to Jennifer, her problems seem to multiply as the days go by and, let's not take this lightly, these are VERY serious problems.

The boss was on her case about a presentation that needed to be done, she had a little ping in her car that was driving her nuts, her boyfriend wanted to go out with his buddies later that night for their annual Fantasy Football draft, her mom was on her case about something that she'd already forgotten and her dog had a little personal hygiene problem that was making her life miserable.

From the point of view of her closest friends, Jennifer's life was paradise. But when she looked in the mirror, she clearly didn't see the person she wanted to see.

For a person like Jennifer, it just appeared as if nothing could make her happy. Not her job, not her friends, not her family. From the outside, she had it all. From behind her big baby blues, she was a wreck.

Then I introduced her to what I call the "The Big Rock Game." Play it. Nothing is simpler. Nothing is more emotionally settling.

I love the Big Rock Game. It's a great quick method for getting your priorities in order and for giving you a better approach to the way you live your everyday life.

When done properly, it also helps people like Jennifer to understand how good her life really is – even when you think you're having nothing but trouble.

Here's how to play:

Take all your big "rocks" out of your pocket and lay them on the table. OK, so you don't have to have real rocks, but it's more fun that way.

In lieu of real rocks, let's grab a sheet of paper and cut it into five or six large "rocks."

On each of the big rocks, just write the five or six things that are the most important parts of your life – to you. Not what you think other people might think, but to you.

For the sake of this particular game, I'm going to list off Jennifer's big rocks:

1. Family – From Your Grand Parents to siblings to Kids
2. Health – From your weight to your ability to sleep at night.
3. Professional – Job, career or school
4. Friends – Both Male and Female
5. Spouse – boyfriend or girlfriend

For Jennifer, she had to quit worrying about all the small rocks and look clearly and honestly at where she stood with her big rocks.

When she did, she found that looking into the mirror every morning became less and less a struggle and more and more a pure, pleasant experience.

Jennifer looked at her big rocks and smiled.

Rock No.1 Family:

"Well, my family's good," she said. "My mom and dad are healthy. My brother is doing well. He's always happy."

Jennifer looked at the big issues and she realized that even though her mom had been on her case more than usual lately, she is extremely fortunate to have a mother who is close to her and wants the best for her. She knows other people who are in much worse situations with their parents

Rock No. 1: Off the table.

When she got to Rock No. 2, she winced.

"I'm healthy, but I have 10 pounds I'd like to lose."

So lose all 10 pounds. Go to bed a little earlier at night and get up in the morning and start exercising. Eat better. If you're overeating or bingeing, then sit down and get a grip on your bad habits. Exercise, eat right, have a good breakfast. Losing 10 pounds isn't all that difficult. If you have your basic health, then weight loss undertaken slowly and properly with exercise and better eating habits, is the easiest thing in the world.

See your doctor. Talk to a nutritionist. Join a gym. Get up half an hour earlier and go for a walk and then later, maybe a run. If you're worried about your food intake, do two simple things: eat less, move more. Consult the national food guide. There are more than enough resources to help you lose weight.

And stop worrying about losing weight tomorrow. It took you longer than a day to put on the weight; it's a guarantee, that it will take some time to take it off. Especially, if you want to remain healthy when the weight's gone. Set goals and start today.

Commit – and I mean commit! – to changing your lifestyle.

Rock No.2: With a game plan to commit to what Jen already knows, No. 2 comes off the table.

Rock No. 3. This is one that really bothered Jennifer.

She realized the only way she would be happy in her professional life was to take steps to change her career. She realized that she was in this career for the money, not love and happiness and love and happiness had to take the lead, not the wages. In fairness, she was in this career because she thought it was right for her. Six years later, even though she was making great wages and had been promoted several times, she was not excited or even motivated to go to the office anymore.

We all have choices in life. Everything we do in our lives is based on our attitude and the choices we make. Jennifer was asked if her career in any way, made her outwardly miserable – if it negatively affected her attitude?

"Every day," she said. "I'm miserable. It's an effort for me to get up in the morning. I'm always out of sorts and I often snap at people. I'm just not happy."

How many times have we heard that in a day? In Jennifer's case, her attitude might have as much to do with her problems at work – and maybe her problems with her boyfriend, her family and her good friends – as anything they've ever done to her.

For Jennifer, there is a big decision to be made here. Rock No. 3 is a big one and it might be the one that affects everything else she does in her life. She has a choice.

A) She can change her attitude toward her job. She can go to work with renewed commitment. She can list all the positives at her workplace and focus on them. Start treating people like they were the most important people in the world and pay no attention at all to the negative aura that seems to be part and parcel of her many other work environments. She can get up early and workout, have a great breakfast and start reading positive and uplifting works that make her happy and give her an emotional boost. She can make the choice that doing her job the way she believes it should be done is more important than worrying about anything else in the work place.

B) She can quit.

Now, we all know that quitting a job can be an extremely difficult thing to do. We keep hearing about how incredibly tough it is to find work. We all can get in a rut disguised as our comfort zone. We have all heard that if you have a well paying job, no matter how horrible it is, you hold onto it with dear life.

Depending on where you live and what you do – there is no question that high-paying jobs are hard to find, you might just want to look at Plan A and say, "That's exactly what I need to do."

However, after giving Plan A a try – and we believe Plan A is a terrific first step, because it IS the 10th Degree – you may find that outside forces have created a poisoned atmosphere in which to work. We won't argue that some bosses can be impossible to work for. Some people are just miserable and those people want to shed their misery on you.

We also know that some jobs are simply places to "get a cheque," every two weeks and provide workers with absolutely no quality of life for eight or nine hours a day.

If it has reached that stage, then quitting might be the only choice Jennifer has. She must weigh the pros and cons of her decision, but it is a choice and if a renewed 10th Degree attitude can't change the abuse that is hurled upon her by a boss or a group of co-workers who cannot and will not live the 10th Degree life, then perhaps it's time to find a new workplace or career.

Granted it takes a great deal of confidence and a commitment to get onto the web, check the job sites, make contact with a headhunter and make a thorough search for available jobs. Fortunately, Jennifer's skills allowed her to find work elsewhere. While she still needed to embrace her physical mastery, mental mastery, emotional mastery and relationship mastery with a little more gusto, she was able to reconcile her professional mastery.

Of course, she had one major concern about any professional step she might take. Money.

Obviously, that is the one other concern with Rock No. 3. Without a job or, at least, a business venture, there is no money.

So where did Jennifer stand in terms of her bank account – and her future bank accounts?

"I'm not where I want to be," she said. "I'm now in my late 20s, I don't really have a lot of money put away, although I have saved some for a down payment on a new car. I want to travel more, but I just don't make enough to do that more than once a year and I know that I have to start putting money away for my future. This is something I need to address."

Because Jennifer isn't burdened by a lot of debt, she's probably in better shape than she believes. But she is approaching her 30s and she needs to make some choices. And remember, we have choices to make every single day.

If she decides to stay with the company that now employs her, Jennifer might have a pension by the time she reaches the age of 60 or 65. Because government pension plans don't pay near enough money to take care of a person in her golden years, it's time for Jennifer to start thinking about a plan. She not only needs a real savings plan for today, but also a pension plan for the future. It's time to call a professional – and as much as you love him, not your dad.

By staying out of crippling debt, Jennifer has a leg up on her money concerns. Call in a professional: a trusted banker or an investment expert with good references and a solid track record, and start preparing for the future. Even if that future is just next month.

A great way to live a 10th Degree life is to get your finances in order and have a plan for the future. Jennifer immediately made a few calls and began taking care of Rock No. 3. She wrote out a plan highlighting the steps she needed to take and she commited herself to follow that plan and re-visit it daily.

For the time being, Jennifer decided to leave Rock No. 3 on the table and move on to Rock No. 4: Her friends.

"My friends? Oh, no problem there," she said, smiling. "I have great friends. I have Dani and Cindy to play golf with, I have Melissa and Jill to party with, I have Marty and Carla in book club and Marie and Kim at the gym. I'm all set."

Terrific, treat your friends like the people they are, the most important people in the world. Rock No. 4 off the table.

And now on to Rock No. 5: Your spouse, or in this case, her boyfriend.

For a moment, that seemed to be an interesting dynamic. Not disturbing, but complicated. Greg didn't always do the things Jennifer wanted him to do.

"My boyfriend? I love him, but well," she hesitated. "OK he's a guy, but he loves me and treats me well and we're honest with each other so even though I'd prefer he didn't go to his stupid Fantasy Football Draft, I went out with the girls after work on Friday night and he didn't complain, so who am I to complain?"

Right, we'll file this one under "Not an issue." Pretty clearly, there is no real problem there. Smile, enjoy life.

Rock No. 5 off the table.

As you can see, the answer to almost all of life's pressing questions can be answered simply be committing to living a 10th

Degree life.

However, whenever you feel you've missed something or are not sure what it is that is bothering you, or you just need a boost, or if the problems of everyday life are getting you down and negatively affecting the way you approach your daily routine, just sit down and play the Big Rock Game.

Chances are, you'll find that your problems are small, your 10th Degree life is, as always, on the right track and that you're a lot better off than you think.

GLEN DAMAN'S LIST

Here are 30 things to remember that will lead you to the 10th Degree.

1. Life is a gift with no receipt so make it the best you can and be thankful for every minute.
2. Don't let yesterday's mistakes ruin your today. There is a reason it's considered the past, learn from it then move on and enjoy the moment. The current moment.
3. No matter our tragedy, time heals sorrow. The healing starts immediately.
4. Read something inspirational and motivational daily.
5. The one thing that can free us from strife and pain is love.
6. You don't have to be successful or wealthy to get started on a 10th Degree life. But you do have to get started.
7. It's never too late to say I'm sorry.
8. In the game of life being right is often different than winning. We must decide is it more important to be right or to win?
9. The greatest day of your life happens more than once.

10. Fate introduces a couple, love keeps you together.

11. Your arms can pick someone up once or twice, but your words can lift them forever.

12. If you knew that the moment you were in would create a powerful memory, would you savor it more?

13. Living life without dreaming is like a river basin without water, empty and still.

14. Remember, unlike theatre there are no dress rehearsals. This is your life. Make every moment count.

15. The best words never came from a pen but from the heart.

16. If you can't tell the ones you love your doing it, then you shouldn't.

17. Don't compare yourself to anyone. Use your own talents to the fullest potential.

18. All smiles are beautiful. Use yours.

19. For the ones that are important to you, hug longer, squeeze tighter and never forget to say I love you.

20. To die with a million friends would make you wealthier than dying with a million dollars

21. Smile before you sleep and when you wake up.

22. Miracles happen every day so take notice.

23. Tell your kids you love them everyday no matter how young or old.

24. Communication is the key to success, never stop trying.

25. Treat your body like a temple you're going to need it.

26. Do something physical for a minimum of 20 minutes everyday

27. If we all do kind deeds for complete strangers, we can change the world.

28. Never be ashamed to cry.

29. Laugh often.
30. Burn the candles, use the nice sheets, open that bottle of wine. Don't save it for a special occasion. Today is that day. Live today, love today.

YOUR FIVE QUICK TIPS TO A 10TH DEGREE LIFE EVERY SINGLE DAY

1. Exercise every morning. The earlier, the better, then have a great breakfast to start the day.
2. Begin every day with focus. Even if you know it's going to be a difficult day, focus in on what needs to be done and get it done. Focus, focus, focus.
3. Read something motivational and inspirational every day. Avoid the newspapers, unless it's the sports section – and, hey, even that can be a downer these days. Read something that makes you happy and gives you a solid, positive outlook to start the day. If you feel you're getting down, read something positive and inspirational again.
4. Eat right. Drink plenty of water. Get a copy of your National Food Guide (we have included Canada's Food Guide in this book) and live by it.
5. At the end of the day, think long and hard about this before nodding off to sleep. The best thing about today was... and then fill in the blank.

YOU'RE HERE: WELCOME TO THE 10TH DEGREE

Someone once told me, "In the race for success there is no finish line."

This is true for the 10th Degree. It takes a lot of hard work, discipline and dedication to get here and it takes the same to remain.

A hockey coach once told a team that I played on that we had to keep doing the things we did to get us here. So true. He also said, "Only practice when you want to win."

Remember, however, that the 10th Degree means enjoying every day and having a 10th Degree attitude means raising the level of the people around you. Enjoy every day and love life.

Life is broken down to the second. Savor everyone of those seconds. It has been said that we only live once, so live life to its fullest. Life has no practice rounds, no dress rehearsals. So live now for the moment you're in.

Love now with no fear. Welcome to The 10th Degree.

THANK YOU

There are too many people to thank. In fact, the entire list
would be another book!

So I thank all my friends. You know who you are. I truly cherish our friendship. However, the following people I had to single out:

Mom, you were and always will be my voice of reason. There truly are no words that can do justice to the way I feel. "Momma's boy" is not a nickname of which I'm ashamed.

Dad, thank you for today and beyond. I look forward to our talks, laughs and tears.

Dad Duckett, thank you for accepting a young boy into your family and always supporting the decisions I made along the way.

Gordon. You are what a big brother should be. There when I need you, always. Thank you.

Karen, my little big sister, and the sounding board, even when it didn't make sense, you listened.

My uncles Len and Chris, thank you, always, for being there.

Bob, you have always said yes, no matter the time or the day. You got me through the school years and now the dad and husband years. Thanks for being my life coach.

Darrell, thank you for the breakfast that changed my life.

Ashok, thank you for all that you taught me.

Scotty thanks for putting all this on paper. You have been very patient and encouraging. Thank you for being a friend.

Everyone at Winnipeg Hyundai, you are like my family away from home. Thank you.

- Glen Daman

TESTIMONIALS

Hi Glen,

After seeing you speak and sitting down with you, talking about living a 10th Degree life, I began my journey up the mountain.

The first and most dramatic change was conquering physical mastery. Getting up early and getting the blood pumping has helped me in every aspect of my life and it's definitely helped me through the other levels of mastery.

With more energy, confidence and an overall feeling of well-being, I have been able to make real, positive changes in my life. In my opinion you have to start with the stepping stone of physical mastery to have the courage and energy to make it up that 10th Degree mountain, and when you do..... WHAT A VIEW!

It has changed my life!

Thank you isn't enough!

Brent

Glen,

While attending your conference approximately a year and half ago, I became totally engaged by your passion and enthusiasm for motivational speaking in particular the 60 Minutes to Success Program to improve your physical and mental well-being.

When I returned home after the seminar I thought, why not give it a try. Well, I have been it doing ever since and not only does it set the tone for my day by getting my blood pumping in the morning, it also prepares me mentally to face the challenges of my day.

After doing this program for a month I noticed immediate changes . Now, when I roll into work, and my attitude has gone from, "Oh well another work day," to "WOW! It's Monday lets get it done!"

Our sales numbers at work have increased and my family has benefited as well. Just so you know, I'm in my fifties and have years of experience traveling on the road of life and that road gets a lot easier to travel when you have a tune up.

I've had the tune up - Thanks to you Glen.

Sincerely,
Vance